EDGAR ALLAN POE—AN AMERICAN IMAGINATION

Kennikat Press
National University Publications
Literary Criticism Series

General Editor
John E. Becker
Fairleigh Dickinson University

EDGAR ALLAN POE
AN AMERICAN IMAGINATION
Three Essays

ELIZABETH PHILLIPS

National University Publications
KENNIKAT PRESS // 1979
Port Washington, N. Y. // London

Manufactured in the United States of America

Published by
Kennikat Press Corp.
Port Washington, N.Y. / London

Library of Congress Congress Cataloging in Publication Data

Phillips, Elizabeth, 1919–
    Edgar Allan Poe, an American imagination.

    (Literary criticism series) (National university
publications)
    Includes bibliographical references
    1. Poe, Edgar Allan, 1809–1849 –Criticism and
interpretation. I. Title.
PS2638.P47   818'.3'09   79-4567
ISBN 0-8046-9216-5

For Vera and Arnold Phillips

CONTENTS

ACKNOWLEDGMENTS

Generous in both their judgments and suggestions with respect to the conceptual aims of this study, Eva Rodtwitt, Eric W. Carlson, and Nancy Cotton merit special thanks. For encouragement and help I am also grateful to Mildred Garris, Edwin G. Wilson, Thomas E. Mullen, Henry S. Stroupe, Will Ray, Kenneth Cherry, Louise Gossett, Thomas F. Gossett, Georgianne McVay, Edward Lobb, Emily Wilson, Andrew Ettin, and Stephanie Roth-Crossland.

I am indebted to Wake Forest University for the Research and Publication Fund from which I have received financial support to see me through the work. I appreciate, too, the cooperation of the library staff, the considerations of my colleagues, and the interest of students in the course of my writing about Poe.

Acknowledgment is made, finally, for permission to quote from the following:

John H. B. Latrobe letter to George W. Eveleth, dated 1852 Dec. 7, location of original of which is not known, but photostat of a copy of which was made for John H. Ingram by Eveleth in 1878 and is in Ingram-Poe Collection, Manuscripts Department, University of Virginia Library; Wallace Stevens, *The Collected Poems,* copyright 1923, 1931, 1935, 1936, 1937, 1942, 1943, 1944, 1945, 1946, 1947, 1948, 1949, 1950, 1951, 1952, 1954 by Wallace Stevens, published by Alfred A. Knopf, Inc.; Wallace Stevens, *The Necessary Angel,* copyright 1942, 1944, 1947, 1948, 1949, 1951 by Wallace Stevens, published by Alfred A. Knopf, Inc.; Wallace Stevens, *Opus Posthumous,* copyright 1957 by Elsie Stevens and Holly Stevens, published by Alfred A. Knopf, Inc.; Alexis de Tocqueville, *Democracy in America,* edited by Phillips Bradley, copyright 1945 by Alfred A. Knopf, Inc.; William Carlos Williams, *Collected Earlier Poems,* copyright 1938 by New Directions Publishing Corporation, reprinted by permission of New Directions; and William Carlos Williams, *In the American Grain,* copyright 1925 by James Laughlin, reprinted by permission of New Directions.

EDGAR ALLAN POE—AN AMERICAN IMAGINATION

ABOUT THE AUTHOR

Elizabeth Phillips is a professor of English at Wake Forest University in Winston-Salem, North Carolina. She is the author of various poems and articles in scholarly journals. Her residence abroad, particularly in England, France and Norway, as well as in the Orient, stimulated her interest in what is American about American literature.

Abbreviations used in Text

H   James A. Harrison, ed., *The Complete Works of Edgar Allan Poe*
J   David K. Jackson, *Poe and the Southern Literary Messenger*
M   Thomas Ollive Mabbott, ed., *Collected Works of Edgar Allan Poe: Poems*
O   John Ward Ostrom, ed., *The Letters of Edgar Allan Poe*

INTRODUCTION

Edgar Allan Poe lived in the imagination, and for that we value him. He also lived in a time and place that was neither a dreamland nor a writer's colony, but a nineteenth-century, provincial America. We have tended to think he was not at home there.

Whatever the intellectual and literary resources, whatever conceptions he worked up, Poe usually knew where he was, had a genuine respect for fact, and was engaged in calculating the chances of selling work he wrote and being a serious man of letters at the same time. When he boasted that the bug ("The Gold-Bug") beat the bird ("The Raven") all hollow,[1] he couldn't have sounded more like us—a little vulgar and more than a little proud. And idiosyncratic as he was, he not only belonged to a new world but was cognizant of it.

Early in his career he wrote that

> nothing but the most egregious national vanity would assign us a place, in the matter of Polite Literature, upon a level with the elder and riper climes of Europe, the earliest steps of whose children are among the groves of magnificently endowed Academies, and whose innumerable men of leisure, and of consequent learning, drink daily from those august fountains of inspiration which burst around them everywhere from out the tombs of their immortal dead, and from out their hoary and trophied monuments of chivalry and song.[2]

It is hardly an exaggeration to say that he has been considered our tragic Miniver Cheevy, who loved the days of old, mourned romance, cursed the commonplace, and eyed a khaki suit with loathing. Although he served in the United States Army for more than a year and a half from May 1827 to December 1828, we doubt that he appreciated the fact that Washington once crossed the Delaware. Yet Poe thought it objectionable that the first president was depicted wearing a toga in Horatio Greenough's Jovian sculpture (H 11:69), and commented that the man who wanted to codify an American English, Noah Webster, seemed "in his great Dictionary" to have had "an idea of being more English than the English . . ." (H 14:185). Poe had, of course, the scavenger's interest in other cultures and an American's "wasteland" mind that regarded, for example, what he called the "proprieties of place, and especially of time" in interior furnishings as "bugbears." Only the timid, he argued, thought a medley of "arabesques," "antediluvian devices," "the chastity of Ionia," and "the sphynxes of Egypt" to be incongruous (H 2:123).

Although Poe did not limit himself to "indigenous creatures," he was no more averse to using them than he was to using anything else at hand. The bird emblematic of time, in Poe's phrase "eternal Condor years," which displaced "the painted paroquet" — the Carolina painted paroquet? — of childhood in the early poem "Romance," was a new world vulture.[3] The gigantic water lilies that furnish a covert for the narrator-observer in the desolate setting of "Silence — A Fable" may be more real than surreal if one notes John James Audubon's observation on the size of the tiger lily, a species

> which grows in swamps and moist copses, in the Northern and Eastern states, as far as Virginia, as well as in the western prairies, attains a height of four or five feet, and makes a splendid appearance with its numerous large drooping flowers, which sometimes amount to twenty or even thirty on a single stem.[4]

The play with the question of who is and who is not a Mason in the story "The Cask of Amontillado" may have been suggested by the fact that membership in the secret Masonic order provoked widespread political controversy culminating in formation of a national Anti-Masonic Party (on whose ticket William Wirt, one of Poe's early benefactors, had run for president of the United States in 1831). Comparing the phenomenon of the maelström off the coast of the Lofoten Islands with "the mighty cataract of Niagara," in "A Descent into the Maelström," Poe reverses at least one American's description of the Niagara whirlpool as "resembling very much, in its appearance and gyrations, the celebrated Maelström on the coast of Norway."[5] When Poe in "Landor's Cottage" remarks on a late evening's smoky mist, he is reminded of Indian summer, a weather condition occurring in the United States and Canada; when he describes an overgrown glade as open enough for the passage of "a Virginia mountain wagon — the most aspiring vehicle . . . of its kind," the humor is home-grown; when he praises the beauty of trees, he names native species, including the magnificent hickories, a triple-stemmed tulip or magnolia, the gentle elm, sassafras and locust, the softer linden, redbud and maple, an occasional silver willow or white poplar; and when he observes a landscape without a fence or "artificial enclosure," he is not in a foreign country. There has been, of course, more than one effort to point out Poe's reliance on the data of experience or awareness of his own time and place; it should hardly be necessary to multiply the examples except for the persistent view that art was more "real" for him than "sensate reality." Bereft of primary resources, Poe would have been merely an epigone. The tensions between what Wallace Stevens calls the collateral text of life and the mind that perceives the life generate the individual character as well as the power of Poe's art, the work of the imagination.

Anticipating the publication of the early volume, *Al Aaraaf, Tamerlane, and Minor Poems* (1829), Poe wrote to a friend: "I would give the world to embody half the ideas afloat in my imagination" (O 1:32). From that time until he died (1849), both the poetry and the prose he wrote would confirm a basic principle: imagination was a liberty of the mind. The final statement of the principle evolved during the course of Poe's work as a critic, and it was not until 1845 that he said, "The range of imagination is . . . unlimited. Its materials extend throughout the universe" (H 12:39, 15:14).

Freedom to range, however, did not mean absolute freedom. The terms within which the freedom was conceived can be observed in his comments on Coleridge's axiom that the imagination creates. Having said in 1831 that he could only speak of Coleridge "with reverence" (H 7:xliii), Poe commented in 1836 that the "imagination is, possibly in man, a lesser degree of the creative power in God." Then he took issue with Coleridge: "What Deity imagines *is*, but *was* also. The mind of man cannot imagine what *is not*." The italics are Poe's: his remarks are in a footnote to a critical essay on Joseph Rodman Drake and Fitz-Greene Halleck, comtemporary poets (H 8:283). The essay itself is of interest for the observation that Shelley had used some physical elements "collaterally" in the illustration of the nature of the Fairy in *Queen Mab*, because the point prepares for further development of Poe's theory of the dependence of the imagination on what *is* or what is known. Moreover, Poe did not continue to defer to Coleridge's views.

By 1840 he disagreed unequivocally with "the dogmatism of Coleridge," who had made an accepted distinction that "the fancy combines, the imagination creates." Poe asserted that "the fancy as nearly creates as the imagination; and neither creates in any respect." He argued that "all novel conceptions are merely combinations. The mind of man can *imagine* nothing which has not really existed; and this point is susceptible of the most positive demonstrations. . . ." Assuming disagreement with the point, he continued:

> It will be said, perhaps, that we can imagine a *griffin*, and that a griffin does not exist. Not the griffin certainly, but its component parts. It is a mere compendium of known qualities. Thus with all which seems to be *new* — which appears to be a *creation* of the intellect. It is resoluble into the old. The wildest and most vigourous effort of the mind cannot stand the test of this analysis. [The italics are again Poe's; the statements are in a discussion of Thomas Moore (H 10:62).]

In 1845 Poe dared to call the principles "New Views" and repeated them with minor variations such as "The mind of man can *imagine* nothing which does not exist: — if it could, it would create not only ideally, but substantially, as do the thoughts of God" (H 12:37). By that time he also was speaking of the "preposterously anomalous metaphysicianism of Coleridge" (H 12:13). Poe's orientation was radical,[6] but came to be accepted by later poets writing about how they work.

Another celebrant of the freedom of the imagination, Wallace Stevens, for example, shared Poe's view of the act of "making" and his criticism of Coleridge's theories. Stevens, like Poe, paid tribute to Coleridge and then disagreed with him: "As poetry goes, as the imagination goes, as the approach to truth, or say, to being by way of the imagination goes, Coleridge is one of the great figures." Even so, Stevens held, "we find in Coleridge . . . a man who may be said to have been defining poetry all his life in definitions that are valid enough, but no longer impress us by their validity." Stevens, also like Poe, theorized about the bounds of the imagination: "There is a limit to its power, . . . and that limit is to be found in nature." Stevens insisted that the "imagination is able to manipulate nature by creating three legs and five arms, but it is not able to create a wholly new nature, as for instance, a new element with creatures indigenous thereto, their costumes and cuisines." Stevens, then, agreed with Poe that the imagination depends on what exists, and is free only to work collaterally with elements of the known world.[7] But Poe said it first.

There is still the question of apprehending the elements and qualities Poe chose from what he knew. The example of a griffin belies the difficulties of analysis, difficulties which follow from the acts of imagination according to Poe's own account: "As often analogously happens in physical chemistry, so not unfrequently does it occur in this chemistry of the intellect, that the admixture of two elements will result in something that shall have nothing of the quality of one of them — or even nothing of the qualities of either" (H 12:38-39). Defining the process by which a poet's mind transmutes materials, T. S. Eliot also makes what he calls "a suggestive analogy" with "the action which takes place when a bit of finely filiated platinum is introduced into a chamber containing oxygen and sulphur dioxide" to "form sulphurous acid" which "contains no trace of platinum." He remarks also that the mind of the poet is a finely perfected medium in which feelings "are at liberty to enter into new combinations."[8]

Since the imagination enjoys the freedom it does and is capable of effecting such changes in the elements — the feelings, the images, the materials — to form new compounds, how can Poe's combinations be discussed except as themselves? Poe, in a period before the rise of realism, critically opposed the proliferation of topical allusion, deliberately held observations of social circumstances and local detail to a minimum for the purpose of idealizing reality, and liked literary subterfuge — all of which increase the problems of analyzing determinants in his transfigurations. Taking him at his word, however, I propose to explore relationships between the world he knew and the combinations which left some traces of the elements he idealized.

I assume that the known world for Poe's conscious and unconscious achievement was not unlike that for other writers: society — for Poe, a democratic culture in which he invested his imagination; a geographical place — the American landscape; and the private or personal life — the "household events" (to use a phrase from Poe's story "The Black Cat"). The subject of mania is the troublesome variable.

Poe's significance as a writer who imaginatively explored psychological states has tended to point his readers away from that portion of his ground, American society which was a consequence of the idea of democracy. Both Poe's theory of literature and reputed aversion to democracy have been used to reinforce the view that he was — in T. S. Eliot's words — "a displaced European."[9] Poe's definition and practice of literature as the idealization of reality is little more European than is the practice and theory of realism, naturalism, or many of the other "isms" including Freudianism, Marxism, or structuralism, which Americans have adapted. The age of realism as well as Freudianism contributed to the difficulties of "assimilating" Poe's work into our literary beginnings. Yet Poe belonged to a period during which a young republic groped to achieve both independence and recognition in literature; he participated actively in the struggle from the outset of his career. In the "Letter to B —," written as a preface for the 1831 edition of *Poems*, Poe complained:

You are aware of the great barrier in the path of an American writer. He is read, if at all, in preference to the combined and established wit of the world. I say established; for it is with literature as with law or empire — an established name is an estate in tenure, or a throne in possession. Besides, one might suppose that books, like their authors, improve by travel — their having crossed the sea is, with us, so great a distinction. Our antiquaries abandon time for distance; our very fops glance from the binding to the bottom of the title-page, where the mystic characters which spell London, Paris, or Genoa, are precisely so many letters of recommendation. . . . [H 7:36]

Was Poe, in the struggle to be read and to become recognized, concerned with relationships between his theory of literature and American political or social phenomena? How did he work from the given reality?

The land within which a society is located is also pertinent to the qualities of a writer's images and ambience. Poe wrote once to John Allan on July 26, 1829, of having gone by foot from Baltimore to Washington and returning the same way. He could hardly have daydreamed incessantly or caroused all the way; he must have looked about him and seen the country. As a young man, at least, he shared the "worship of nature" which was one of the prime movers of the romantic spirit; and attention has been given to his interest in the aesthetics of landscape painting. What use did Poe make of his experience of the American landscape, the locale, not just as "a decorative embellishment" but as an integral or aggregate subject?

After considering Poe's imagined landscapes, I have asked what Poe knew about himself in regard to one major personal problem for which there is some extra-literary information. Questioning whether or not the stories depicting deranged states of mind are directly autobiographical, I work from the evidence of his correspondence in relation to the fact that he was a man who had a history of alcoholism with concomitant psychological disturbances which the letters at least outline. How did he conceive the difficulties, and what was there available to him for an understanding of the problem which persisted throughout his adult life? What did Poe and Poe's contemporaries know about the latent springs and manifest perversions of the human mind? What did Poe make of the knowledge? What is its bearing on the course of both an imagination and destiny that are still enigmatic?

Whether Poe has been viewed disparagingly or sympathetically as a man who suffered a disconnection between inner and outer worlds, he has been America's imaginative man who sought to detach himself from "earthly things," or preferred supernal beauty, the dream, the remote scene, perhaps even hated contact with reality, and without a doubt hated the America in which he was born. He has been given a French face, a British tradition, and a Germanic mind. We see the provincial Poe but never fully see the relation between the world in which he lived — a new world — and that imagination which sought to collate the lines that were intelligible to him. I hope, however, that further study of three discrete subjects which prescribed the freedom of his imagination and shaped much of Poe's work can add to our understanding of the strengths as well as the weaknesses of his literary achievement in a new world.

THE AIR OF DEMOCRACY
AND THE IMAGINATION OF MAN

"... the imagination and society are inseparable."
Wallace Stevens
"The Noble Rider and the Sound of Words"

"The strong sense of a beginning in Poe is in no one
else before him. What he says, being thoroughly local
in origin, has some chance of being universal in application. . . . He is American. . . ."
William Carlos Williams
In the American Grain

1

"I readily admit that the Americans have no poets; I cannot allow that they have no poetic ideas." This double-edged remark by Alexis de Tocqueville in *Democracy in America*[1] could well have been the provocation of an acute and poignant defense of America by Poe in 1842. Poe had earlier in the year resigned as editor of *Graham's Magazine* where he had been admirably enterprising in the nation's struggle for literary independence. He chose the introduction to a review, published in November 1842, of Rufus Griswold's *Poets and Poetry of America* for a discussion germane to Tocqueville's classic work on the relation of political and social phenomena to the development of a culture.

Although neither the French author's name nor his work is mentioned, Tocqueville's views were in the air and Poe appeals to the readers' familiarity with the issues — the book had been eagerly read and debated in France, England, and the United States. By 1845 it had been adopted for use in American schools, but whether Poe himself ever read it is impossible to say.

Since the First Part of *Democracy in America* (1835) had been devoted to the political character, the virtues, and anomalies of the democratic government of the United States, the Second Part (1840) was an inquiry into the civil aspect of the nation. In considering the consequences of the American political experiment, Tocqueville examined "the action of the intellect" and speculated on the sources of poetry among a democratic people. Poets, for Tocqueville, delineated the ideal, and democracy created a change of circumstances as well as difficulties for the realization of imaginative ideas. Tocqueville observed that "in democracies the love of physical gratification, the notion of bettering one's condition, the excitement of competition, the charm of anticipated success are so many spurs to urge men onward in the active professions they have embraced . . ." (2:75-76). The American imagination, he said, "is not extinct, but its chief function is to devise what may be useful and to represent what is real." Such a climate was not salutary, even if it were not miasmic, for poetry as Tocqueville conceived of it.

Poe kept an eye on the weather and the national reputation. "That we are not a poetical people," he began the review of Griswold's book, "has been asserted so often and so roundly, both home and abroad, that the slander, through mere dint of repetition, has come to be received as truth" (H 11:147-49). The mistaken opinion, Poe explained, was a corollary of the old dogma which held "the calculating faculty" to be "at war with the ideal. . . ." The two divisions of the mental powers, he argued, were "never to be found in perfection apart." For Poe, "the *highest* order of the imaginative intellect is always preeminently mathematical; and the converse." Poe's solution to the dilemma of the poet, then, was to shift the grounds; his poet would not sacrifice one cognitive power to the other, but effect a union of faculties to cope with the American circumstances. The rapprochement made it possible to agree and to disagree with a Tocquevillian characterization of the air of democracy.

Poe, like Tocqueville, addressed himself to the historical preoccupations of the young country. Poe mentioned "the idiosyncrasy of the American political position" which had "stimulated into early action whatever political talent we possessed"; the "utilitarian ability" evinced "in our national infancy"; achievements "in all the arts and sciences which promote the *comfort* of the animal man"; and the fact that the "distinction, in which our first and most obvious wants impelled us, has been regarded as the field of our deliberate choice." Poe was, of course, arguing a personal cause, but there was nothing peculiarly impertinent in that. "Our necessities," he pleaded, "have been mistaken for our propensities. Having been forced to make railroads, it has been deemed impossible that we should make verse. . . . Because we were not all Homers in the beginning, it has been somewhat too rashly taken for granted that we shall be all Jeremy Benthams in the end." Tocqueville's analysis was not, just here, at issue, and Poe had not necessarily misrepresented that analysis. He had, rather, adapted Tocqueville's kinds of observations to support the development of American literature.

Tocqueville's discussion of the sources of poetry among a democratic people was preceded by a report on the literary characteristics of the "times." The "times" were ambiguously both the period of his visit to America from May 1831 to February 1832 and the date of publication of his study in 1840. "The inhabitants of the United States," Tocqueville noted without regard for a decade that was important in the country's cultural naissance, "have . . . at present, properly speaking, no literature." Tocqueville contended, however, that if the Americans, "retaining the same laws and social conditions had had a different origin and had·been transported into another country," they would have had a literature. "Even as they are," he predicted with ease, "I am convinced that they will ultimately have one . . ." (2:58-59). Tocqueville did not know about Poe.

"The principles of the poetic sentiment," Poe continued in the apologia of 1842, "lie deep within the immortal nature of man, and have little necessary reference to the worldly circumstances which surround him. The poet in Arcady is, in Kamschatka, the poet still." Then Poe (Irish and English in descent) pivoted to Tocqueville's curious view of "origin," and made the point that the "self-same Saxon current animates the British and American heart; nor can any social, or political, or moral, or physical conditions do more than momentarily repress the impulses which glow in our bosoms as fervently as in those of our progenitors." Tocqueville, as he said, was interested in the impact of those repressive conditions on the poet; but so was Poe. He believed that he could overcome them.

Although he had only three poems in Griswold's 1842 anthology, Poe had published *Tamerlane and Other Poems* in 1827, followed by second and third volumes of poetry in 1829 and 1831. A first group of tales, beginning with "Metzengerstein," was printed in 1832, and by 1840 he had collected a total of twenty-five stories in *Tales of the Grotesque and Arabesque*. Since 1835 he had also been active as a journalist-critic and editor in the cause of American literature. What would have hurt Poe was Tocqueville's distant, casual view. But even if the American writer were cut to the quick, Poe's closer and more accurate view further suggests that his remarks, written in the summer of 1842, over ten years after Tocqueville's visit, could have been a reply to the prophetic text. Poe's authority and faith were his own; he did not live to benefit from the recognition that Tocqueville's country was to give to the man the French thought to be America's first literary genius. And, in the historical cross fire, Tocqueville's study aided Poe's cause in France. "Following the lead of Tocqueville's famous book," as Patrick Quinn points out, "Baudelaire had emphasized the improbability of America's fostering an artistic talent of any real importance."[2] Poe's last words vis-à-vis Tocqueville's observations become, then, especially poignant:

> Those who have taken most careful note of our literature for the last ten or twelve years, will be most willing to admit that *we are* a poetical people; and in no respect is the fact more plainly evinced than in the eagerness with which books professing to compile or select from

the productions of our native bards, are received and appreciated by the public.

Poe then discussed Griswold's compilation of poems.

The careful note which Poe could with reason say he had taken of American poetry when he is compared with Tocqueville, had been preceded by an equally informed note on American letters and criticism. The article, on J. G. C. Brainard's poetry, appeared in *Graham's* issue of February 1842, nine months before the publication of the review of Griswold's anthology; the tone was bold, and the temper was not chauvinistic. Putting the work of the native writers of fiction and verse in historical perspective, Poe explained the habit of apotheosizing "the *pioneers* of American literature," but contended that "we are now strong in our own resources. We have, at length, arrived at that epoch when our literature may and must stand on its merits, or fall through its own defects." Stating that *"at last,* then, we are in a condition to be criticized — even more, to be neglected," he thought the journalist "no longer in danger of being impeached for *lèse majesté* of the Democratic spirit, who shall assert with sufficient humility, that we have committed an error in mistaking Kettell's *Specimens* [of American Poetry, an anthology of inferior verse] for the Pentateuch or Joseph Rodman Drake for Apollo" (H 11:16-17). The apparent willingness to be neglected suggests that Tocqueville's sweeping judgment had not yet come to Poe's attention. His change of attitude, his joining in the defense of his countrymen shortly thereafter, suggests that Poe might have read Tocqueville in the spring or summer of 1842. The review of Griswold's *Poets* was written in midsummer of that year (O 1:211-12).

Poe signaled the change with a careful and informed note assessing American short stories in an essay published in May of the same year, 1842, on Hawthorne's *Twice-Told Tales.* Poe's evaluation, which proved to be astute, affords an immediate parallel to Tocqueville's judgments. "We have," Poe wrote, "very few American tales of real merit — we may say, indeed, none, with the exception of 'The Tales of a Traveller' of Washington Irving, and these 'Twice-Told Tales' of Mr. Hawthorne" (H 11:109-10). Hawthorne's *Scarlet Letter* (1850) had not yet appeared; the stories, in Poe's emphatic opinion, belonged "to the highest region of Art — an Art subservient to genius of a very lofty order." Poe was later, in 1847, to deride the press and the public for scarcely recognizing Hawthorne's work; at the same time Poe also explained Hawthorne's weaknesses and attempted to account for the "inappreciation" (H 13:141-55). He did not, however, change an opinion expressed about Hawthorne's merit in 1842: "We know of few compositions which the critic can more honestly commend than these. . . . As Americans, we feel proud of the book."

Tocqueville's brief look at the literary battleground that was provincial America was not altogether careless. The French observer saw and sympathetically rebuked the continuing dependence of the United States on English literature and taste, two generations after the country had won political independence. A sense of the historical moment was, however, more than academic for Poe. He was the grandson of David Poe, wheelwright and later drygoods merchant, who was active in the American Revolution, was commissioned assistant deputy-quartermaster general (with the rank of major) for the city of Baltimore in 1799, and spent forty thousand silver dollars on the cause of independence. He died in October 1816. The partisan French general Lafayette visited David Poe's grave in Baltimore, and young Edgar was lieutenant of the Junior Volunteers who acted as guard of honor for Lafayette when he visited Richmond in October of 1824. Lafayette was not Tocqueville or Baudelaire's grandfather, but he was a friend of Poe's grandfather. Familial history is no counterbalance to the accepted view of Poe's lack of national feeling; on the other hand, his self-assumed double duty as patriot and critic has not been overstressed: "As Americans, we feel proud of the book." A fine modesty is not supposed to become him; wishful thinking was his forte. Had Tocqueville been only a little more informed about what was happening during the painful beginnings of literary independence — the cause of Poe's generation — Poe would have rejoiced to claim another French ally.

There were, after all, Tocqueville's remarks on the situation in which native authors found themselves. The French visitor noted that most of the books in an American bookseller's shop were written in Europe, that England supplied readers with most of the books they required, that the larger part of the writers in the country were "English in substance and still more so in form," that they transported "into the midst of democracy the ideas and fashions . . . current among the aristocratic nations . . . taken for their model." He further observed that before citizens of the United States could "make up their minds upon the merits of one of their authors," readers generally waited "until his fame" had been "ratified in England." Long before Tocqueville's analysis, Poe commented in 1836 that if Americans "were induced to read at all the productions of our native writers, it was only after repeated assurances from England that such productions were not altogether contemptible" (H 9:276). And in spite of the praise Poe gave American readers when he spoke of their reception of anthologies of poetry, he continued to be legitimately troubled by the problems of the writers' recognition in the United States. Arguing in 1845 for an international copyright law, Poe spoke of the country's being inundated with British opinion in British books, complained that when an American book was published readers turned up their noses until it had been "dubbed 'readable' by some illiterate Cockney critic," and observed "that in the few instances in which our writers have been treated with common decency in England, these writers have either openly paid homage to English institutions, or have had lurking at the bottom of their hearts a secret principle at war with Democracy. . . ."[3] Then, in the spirit of American writers including William Ellery Channing, Henry W. Longfellow, James Fenimore Cooper, and Margaret Fuller, as well as Ralph Waldo Emerson who gave the most felicitous expression to the cause, Poe demanded "the nationality of self-respect," and proclaimed: "In Letters as in Government we require a Declaration of Independence. A better thing still would be a Declaration of War—"

Again, in 1845 Poe argued the question of international copyright which, he said, had been "overloaded with words" (H 16:78-79). He spoke of the injury to the national literature because the efforts of writers of genius were repressed. "Our genius being thus repressed, we are written *at* only by our 'gentlemen of elegant leisure,' and mere gentlemen of elegant leisure have been noted, time out of mind for the insipidity of their productions." He went on to say that in general, too, such men were "obstinately conservative" and that this feeling led them into "imitation of foreign, more especially British models." This, Poe thought, was "one main source of imitativeness with which, as a people, we have been justly charged, although the first cause is to be found in our position as a colony." Furthermore, Poe stated, "irreparable ill is wrought by the almost exclusive dissemination among us of foreign — that is to say, of monarchial or aristocratical sentiment in foreign books; nor is this sentiment less fatal to democracy because it reaches the people themselves in the gilded pill of the poem or novel." Poe spoke also of the "sense of insult and injury aroused in the whole active intellect of the world, the bitter and fatal resentment excited in the universal heart of literature — a resentment which will not and which cannot make nice distinctions between the temporary perpetrations of the wrong and that democracy in general which permits its perpetration." He concluded the argument by assailing "the authorial body" as "the most autocratic on the face of the earth," and asking "How, then, can those institutions [the authorial body, the press, editors, publishers] even hope to be safe which systematically persist in trampling it [democracy] under foot?" Part of Poe's statement has been taken to mean that he was "unhappy" with democracy,[4] but as a whole it is rather a reprimand to those who do not understand the relationship between abuse of freedom and free institutions.

The self-interest and the sense of injustice which give passionate force to Poe's polemics have usually been considered likely motives for his "aversion" to democracy. It is clear, for example, that Poe was as inclined to make observations similar to Tocqueville's as to take issue with his assessments of the situation. Tocqueville himself, reasonable and interested in viewing the American experiment, worried that the time had come when the choice was not between aristocracy or democracy; he feared a choice between, on the one hand, "a democracy without poetry, or elevation indeed," although "with order and morality," and, on the other, "an undisciplined and depraved democracy, subject to sudden frenzies or a yoke heavier than any that had galled mankind since the fall of the Roman Empire" (appendix 2: 402-3). Poe's use of the word "mob" as a pejorative (a sense in which Emerson also used the term) and frequent criticisms of "omniprevalent Democracy" (H 4:203) are commonplaces in many analyses of his work. "Is it, or is it not a fact," Poe wrote in 1849, "that the air of a Democracy agrees better with mere Talent than with Genius?" (H 16:152). The complaint is pointed. Poe embodied the strain between the imagined advantages of a cultural elite and the exigencies of a more egalitarian, mercantile society in which he had to earn his way. He was, after all, the first major American writer who lived almost entirely on the income from the sale of what he wrote. He began as a southern and therefore provincial editor and critic, was hardly accepted in the most powerful, established centers of American culture, but retained notions of personal superiority as well as sympathy with the "aristocratic" South. The southern orientation is associated with English attitudes — Poe was influenced by English literature — and there is, in addition, Poe's interest in European literary ideas.[5] Finally, it is an undisputed fact that Poe refused to support a narrow literary nationalism which praised American writers because they were American. These characteristics are not generally considered to be evidence of Poe's having taken for granted, as it is typical for intellectuals and journalists to do, that the country needed to be criticized. Scarcely anyone dares suggest the likelihood that Poe meant what he said in tirades against those who "had lurking at the bottom of their hearts a secret principle at war with Democracy," who "were obstinately conservative," and of "aristocratical sentiment . . . fatal to democracy."

Whether Poe was aristocratic or democratic in sympathy, however, is not a matter of judging intentions on the basis of one set of pronouncements in contrast to another. William Carlos Williams was probably accurate when he described Poe as both an aristocrat and a democrat.[6] More important than the tensions in Poe's view of himself with respect to class sympathies is the recognition that he was a writer in a democratic society and that he knew it. Studies of his work as journalist-critic and his effort to adapt the British magazine tradition to the American market have made that clear. What, however, was the impact of the idea of democracy itself on the imagination of Poe as a writer who had a cogent awareness of political and social realities for which there was not yet a literary tradition?

2

When Tocqueville said he was convinced that the United States would ultimately have a literature, he added that its character would be different from that of the American literary work in the period about which he was writing, "and that character will be peculiarly its own" (2:59, 63). He warned that he should say more than he meant if he were to assert that the literature of a nation "is always subordinate to its social state and its political constitution." He was "aware that, independently of these causes, there are several others which confer certain characteristics on literary productions," but he gave chief importance to the relations that exist between the social and political conditions of a people and the genius of its authors. Tocqueville, then, made the analysis "Of Some Sources of Poetry among Democratic Nations." While Tocqueville's brilliant studies of the consequences of democracy have been frequently used in books on American art, literature, and culture,[7] no one has hitherto examined the prognostications for literature and the work of Poe. Soothsayer that he was, Tocqueville predicted Poe.

Although Poe's second volume, *Al Aaraaf, Tamerlane, and Minor Poems,* had been printed in 1829, two years before Tocqueville visited the United States, the book had very little sale or attention. Even if, by chance, Tocqueville saw it, he disclaims American work with which he was familiar as a basis of the speculations about literature in a democracy, and it is unlikely that seventeen poems by an unknown young man not yet a professional writer would have stimulated the theories of the French observer. Tocqueville himself attributes the basis of the predictions to the work "of the greatest poets who have appeared since the world turned to democracy" – Goethe's *Faust,* Byron's *Childe Harold,* Chateaubriand's *René,* and Lamartine's *Jocelyn* (2:81). For Poe's part, his direction was clearly established before Tocqueville's analysis was published in 1840; whether Poe had read Tocqueville or not, nothing but the prose-poem *Eureka* (1848) is markedly different enough from work of the thirties to have been in the least influenced by Tocqueville's analysis. Having also read and admired – among others – at least three of the writers that Tocqueville cited, Poe developed nonetheless independently in practice as Tocqueville almost concurrently hypothesized a kind of literature that could be expected.

Tocqueville and Poe held similar conceptions of poetry. For Tocqueville, it was "the search after, and delineation of, the Ideal." "The Poet," he said, "is he who, by suppressing a part of what exists, by adding some imaginary touches to the picture, and by combining certain real circumstances that do not in fact happen together, completes and extends the work of nature." For Tocqueville, "The object of poetry is not to represent what is true, but to adorn it and to present to the mind some loftier image. Verse, regarded as the ideal beauty of language, may be eminently poetical; but verse does not of itself constitute poetry" (2:71). The qualifying remarks about verse, as well as the inclusion of Chateaubriand's tale of *René* in the list of work from which Tocqueville cited new directions, imply that he is considering poetry not as a genre but in the generic sense of literature as a fine art.

When Poe in the early essay (1836) on Joseph Drake and Fitz-Greene Halleck attempted a definition of poetry, as R. D. Jacobs has pointed out, "he formulated a single first principle — that all poetry must be ideal, . . ." and he also took poetry "in its larger sense, as embracing all genres of art."[8] Whatever changes in vocabulary and emphasis Poe made during the years he wrote as a critic, he worked from assumptions that are similar to Tocqueville's. "Were I called on to define, *very* briefly, the term 'Art,' " Poe wrote in 1849, "I should call it 'the reproduction of what the Senses perceive in Nature through the veil of the Soul.' The mere imitation, however accurate, of what *is* in Nature, entitles no man to the sacred name of 'Artist' " (H 16:164). In another discussion of the aim of art (1842), he defined the idealization of the pictorial:

> That the chief merit of a picture is its *truth* is an assertion deplorably erroneous. . . . Indeed it is curious to observe how very slight a degree of truth is sufficient to satisfy the mind, which acquiesces in the absence of numerous essentials in the thing depicted. An outline frequently stirs the spirit more pleasantly than the most elaborate picture. . . . Without even color the most thrilling effects are produced. In statues we are rather pleased than disgusted with *the want of the eyeball*. The hair of the Venus de Medici *was gilded*. Truth indeed! . . . If truth is the highest aim of either Painting or Poesy, then Jan Steen was a greater artist than Angelo, and Crabbe is a more noble poet than Milton. [H 11:84]

Poe's regard for the value of truth in various literary genres other than poetry did not contradict the general first principle of idealization. When Poe spoke of the superiority of the tale "even over the poem," he praised it for its advantage in "the development of all points of thought or expression which have their basis in *Truth*" (H 11:108-9). Truth, he said in the well-known essay on Hawthorne's stories, "is often, and in a very great degree, the aim of the tale." Poe, however, was talking about what Jacobs terms "truth of feeling" (p. 306). To Poe, as Jacobs observes, the poem "could not be the vehicle of any kind of truth other than the truth of feeling." Poe limited poetry to expression of the "sentiment" of the beautiful. "For," he remarked in the essay on Hawthorne, "beauty can be better treated in the poem. Not so with terror, or passion, or horror, or a multitude of such other points" (H 11:109). These feelings could be effected in the tale. Writing about the fiction of Charles Dickens, Poe made it clear that he was not measuring truth by conscientious realism: "No critical principle is more firmly based in reason," he stated, "than that a certain amount of exaggeration is essential in the proper depiction of truth itself. We do not paint an object to be true, but to appear true to the beholder. Were we to copy nature with accuracy the object copied would seem unnatural" (H 10:152-53). Discussing the problems of a poetic drama by Frances Sargent Osgood, Poe again held to the measure: "A greater number of striking points than are ever seen closely conjoined to reality, may, for artistical purposes be gathered into the action of a drama — provided always that there be no absolute controversion of nature's general intention. . . . The drama, in a word, must be truthful without conveying the true . . ." (H 13:113).

Poe's finer distinctions with respect to literary genres do not, then, exclude his prose fiction from an analysis of his achievements compared with what Tocqueville anticipated. If one works from Poe and Tocqueville's assumptions about the nature of literature whose sources and audience are a democratic society, what among the actions, sentiments, and opinions of the people is appropriate to a conception of the ideal? One immediately faces severe difficulty, because as Tocqueville argued, "the taste for ideal beauty, and the pleasures derived from the expression of it, are never so intense or so diffused among a democratic as among an aristocratic people." Not only does the principle of equality divert men from the description of ideal beauty, but it also "diminishes the number of objects to be described." Granted, Poe's stress on "the hedonic value" (Jacobs, p. 17) of poetry as a genre is the reason for his distinction between poem and tale as well as for his stand against didactics and the moral virtues that justified the verse of his contemporaries. His persistence in elaborating a limited or narrow range of subjects, themes, and situations in both the poems and prose fiction, however, is an accepted and valid criticism of Poe as a writer. He, nevertheless, faced a change in historical circumstances that called for ingenuity and imaginative intelligence.

3

Aristocracy, in Tocqueville's view, maintained society in a fixed position, was favorable to the solidity and duration of positive religions, and kept the human mind within a certain sphere of belief. An aristocratic people was always "prone to place intermediate powers between God and man," the universe itself was peopled with supernatural beings, discovered by the mind and available to the poet as subjects in which "a countless audience" took an interest. "In democratic ages, it sometimes happens, on the contrary, that men are as much afloat in matters of faith as they are in their laws." Skepticism then draws the poets back to earth, confines them to the real and visible world, depopulates the heaven, simplifies religious conviction, and diverts attention from secondary agents. If the principle of equality does not disturb religious belief, it tends to fix it primarily on the Supreme Power (2:76). "Democratic poets will always appear trivial and frigid," Tocqueville predicted, "if they seek to invest gods, demons, or angels with corporeal forms and if they attempt to draw them down from heaven to dispute the supremacy of the earth" (2:79-80). The poet, then, "will not attempt to people the universe with supernatural beings, in whom his readers and his own fancy have ceased to believe; nor will he coldly personify virtues and vices, which are better received under their own features. All these resources fail him . . ." (2:80-81).

Although Poe believed in God, he was not a traditional Christian poet.[9] Moreover, he was attentive to the effect of skepticism on the poet. In the "Sonnet — To Science" (1829),[10] he protests that science — knowledge— is a vulture with peering eyes and changes all things in the world of imagination. The vulture preys upon the poet's heart; the vulture's wings are dull realities which the poet does not love; and the rapacious bird will not let the imaginative man wander freely or soar undaunted to seek for treasures in the jeweled skies. The poem, it is true, is not about the loss of Christian faith, but laments the violence science has done to the creatures of ancient mythology: Diana has been dragged from her car, the Hamadryad driven from the wood, the Naiad torn from her flood, the Elfin from the grass — all are gone and with them the poet's summer dream beneath the tamarind tree. This sonnet precedes by a century Wallace Stevens's statement that the death of Satan was a tragedy for the imagination; but Poe shared in the gradual decreation of the powerful images and topography of Christian belief when he published *Al Aaraaf* (1829), a young poet's effort to write a supreme fiction, for which "Sonnet — To Science" was the prefatory note.

The setting of *Al Aaraaf* is the celebrated star that appeared and dis-

appeared suddenly in 1572. For Poe it was "a messenger star of the Deity
. . . on an embassy to our world" (O 1:18). He explains that the poem's
title was "from the Al Aaraaf of the Arabians, a medium between Heaven
and Hell where men suffer no punishment, but yet do not attain that
tranquil and even happiness which they suppose to be characteristic of
heavenly enjoyment" (M 103). It is, as Thomas O. Mabbott has said, "a
place that is not meant to fit into any system of cosmology save one that
Poe imagined" (M 104). A peculiarity of Al Aaraaf, Poe further explains,
is that those who choose to go there "do not enjoy immortality – but
after a second life of high excitement, sink into forgetfulness and death."
Heaven itself bestows neither grace nor hope to lovers on the star. (The
idea, Poe points out, was taken from Job – "I would not live always –
let me alone.") Poe not only forgoes the Christian hope for immortality;
he also refutes the concept of an anthropomorphic God, and quotes
from Charles R. Sumner's *Notes on Milton's Christian Doctrine* as well as
other authorities in a footnote to the effect that to think of God "as
having really a human form" is "one of the most ignorant errors of the
dark ages of the church" (M 103). Poe emphasizes, nevertheless, God's
"vastness and power (not merely in minor things like tempests) and His
omnipresence. . . . Spirits fill happy flowers, and even inanimate sculptures
have flown in spirit to the new star" (M 84).

The poem "Israfel" (1831) comes closer than any in the Poe canon
to what Tocqueville calls peopling Heaven with supernatural beings, but
the motive for the poem is to contrast the mortal world "of sweets and
sours" with the celestial realm of ecstasy and poetic power. Like the
"Sonnet – To Science," "Israfel" is a lament and protest of the poet on
earth, where "our flowers are merely flowers." Even though the poet
longs for inspiration from the spirit of Israfel "whose heart strings are a
lute," Poe neither prays to nor invokes a blessing from the poetic angel.
The poet of earth sings, instead, "a mortal melody."

Poe continued also to object to the idea of an anthropomorphic God.
Criticizing a poem by John G. C. Brainard on "The Fall of Niagara"
(1842), Poe wrote: "It is needless to say . . . that bestowing upon Deity
a human form is at best a low and most unideal conception" (H 11:21).

None of these attitudes owes anything to Tocqueville. But in the same
year that Poe discussed Brainard's poem and Griswold's anthology, he
wrote of Baron de la Motte Fougué's poem *Undine*, with its water sprites
and preternatural creatures, that the pathos, although "truly beautiful and
deep, fails of much of its effect through the material from which it is
wrought. The chief character, being endowed with purely fanciful attributes, cannot command our full sympathies, as can a simple denizen of
the earth" (H 10:154-55). In 1846 he wrote again of the same poem that

it was "exquisite," but "too chilly for our people, and, generally, for our epoch. We have less imagination and warmer sympathies than the age which preceded us."[11] Admirable as the poem was, "Its kind can *never* be appreciated by Americans" (H 16:117). In 1845 he criticized Elizabeth Barrett Browning's *Drama of Exile*, an epic which cited Milton's *Paradise Lost* as one of its models. Poe did not wish, he said, to dwell irreverently on matters which had venerability in the faith and fancy of Miss Barrett. Nevertheless, he found the Christian epic no support for the invisible angels of her poem.

> She has made allusion to Milton. . . . But even in Milton's own day, when men had the habit of believing all things . . . and worshipping, in blind acquiescence, the most preposterous of impossibilities — even *then*, there were not wanting individuals who would have read the great epic with more zest, could it have been explained to their satisfaction, how and why it was, not only that a snake quoted Aristotle's ethics, and behaved otherwise pretty much as he pleased, but that bloody battles were continually being fought between bloodless "innumerable angels," that found no inconvenience in losing a wing one minute and a head the next, and if pounded up into puff-paste late in the afternoon, were as good "innumerable angels" as new the next morning, in time to be at *reveille*. . . . [H 12:7-8]

Such were the limitations of Poe as critic in a period when the Christian images as well as the classical allusions were in the process of losing their vitality.

Poe also objected to personification as a senseless mannerism before he could have possibly read the discussions of sources of poetry among a democratic people. Of the *Last Days of Pompeii*, by Bulwer-Lytton, Poe commented in 1839, "Does he mention 'truth' in the most ordinary phrase? — she is with a great T. Truth, the divinity. All common qualities of the mind, all immaterial or mental existences, are capitalized into persons. . . . [The book] is ridiculously full of it" (H 14:91-92). Poe may have capitalized Hope or Beauty, but he did not personify virtues and vices in the poetry he wrote, and an aesthetic which argued for beauty and the truth of feeling rather than moral truth gave him the confidence to write in "Annabel Lee" (1849) that "neither the angels in Heaven above/ Nor the demons down under the sea/ Can ever dissever my soul from the soul/ Of the beautiful Annabel Lee. . . ." Perhaps the sentiment is a lyrical exaggeration, but he would have us believe that "the winged seraphs of Heaven" coveted the love of the children in that poem. The poem is not a religious but a secular ballad in which human love is idealized and consummated in death. Although a far cry from the loveliness of the lost star described in *Al Aaraaf*, the mortal strains of the two poems are from one voice.

The "gorgeous nonsense" of the ideal world of *Al Aaraaf* prepared, at least in the opinion of one Poe scholar, Floyd Stovall, for the ambitious prose-poem, *Eureka*, which was published in 1848. Compared with the charm of *Al Aaraaf*, however, the vision in *Eureka* is an empty and terrifying abstraction. Mabbott points out that Poe attempted to make his ideas conform to current scientific concepts, as he understood them (p. 94). He calls it a treatise in which a survey of the universe is taken. By the term "universe" he means "to designate the utmost conceivable expanse of space, with all things, spiritual and material, that can be imagined to exist within the compass of that expanse" (H 16:186). The first cause of this universe is God and the universe is a conception, a plot of God, whose original and sole creation was a primordial particle — unified and unparticled because it was, like God himself, spirit, yet it was infinitely divisible; and by an act of volition God diffused the one particle into particles of matter throughout a limited sphere in space to constitute the universe as we now know it, the Universe of Stars. Thus diffused, these particles of matter become subject to the law of gravitation, the effect of which will be that eventually all matter as atomic substance will be annihilated by returning to its original state as unparticled matter, or spirit.

Critics such as Allen Tate and Daniel Hoffman have suggested that there is a relationship between the recurrent subject of disintegration in Poe's tales and the theme of *Eureka:* "In the original unity of first things lies the secondary cause of all things, with the germ of their inevitable annihilation." Tate argues that Poe's characters are machines of sensation and will, with correspondences in the physical universe of particles of energy: both man and the universe are dehumanized. "Poe's engrossing obsession in *Eureka* with the cosmic destiny of man issued in a quasi-cosmology, a more suitable extension of his vision than any mythology, home-made or traditional, could have offered him." The great mythologies, as Tate observes, "are populous worlds, but a cosmology need have nobody in it. In Poe's, the hyperaesthetic egoist has put all other men into his void: he is alone in the world, and thus dead to it."[12] Whether or not *Eureka* is an extension of Poe's psychological subjects, it is with one substantive difference a culmination of a series of attitudes Tocqueville predicted.

If poets, in Tocqueville's view, "strive to connect the great events they commemorate with the general providential designs that govern the universe and . . . reveal the thoughts of the Supreme Mind, their works will be admired and understood..." (2:80). Tocqueville foresaw this conclusion on the basis that democratic man, "raising his eyes about his country, begins at length to discern mankind at large ..." (2:79). At the same time that men look "at the human race as one great whole, they easily conceive that its destinies are regulated by the same design; and in the actions of every individual they are led to acknowledge a trace of that universal and eternal plan by which God rules our race" (2:79). Poe did not "commemorate" great events. There is, however, among the paragraphs he published in 1845 one that prepares readers for *Eureka:*

> In the life of every man there occurs at least one epoch when the spirit seems to abandon, for a brief period, the body, and elevating itself above mortal affairs just so far as to get a comprehensive and *general* view, makes an estimate of its humanity, as accurate as possible to that particular spirit. The soul here separates itself from its own idiosyncrasy, or individuality, and considers its own being, not as appertaining solely to itself, but as a portion of the universal Ens. All the important good resolutions which we keep − all startling, marked regenerations of character − are brought about by these *crises* in life. And thus it is our *sense of self* which debases, and which keeps us debased. [H 14:186]

Having finished *Eureka,* Poe quietly noted afterward in the *Marginalia,* 1849, that "an infinity of error makes its way into our philosophy through Man's habit of considering himself a citizen of a world solely − of an individual planet − instead of at least occasionally contemplating his position as a cosmopolite proper − as a denizen of the universe" (H 16:167).

While Tocqueville could not possibly have influenced the attitudes in Poe's work before 1840, and while Poe did not succeed in connecting the commemoration of great events with the general providential designs that govern the universe, the parallels between the conception of a work like *Eureka* and Tocqueville's predictive work are intriguing.[13] "Think," Poe's prose-poem concludes, "that the sense of individual identity will be gradually merged in the general consciousness; that Man, for example, ceasing imperceptibly to feel himself Man, will at length attain that awfully triumphant epoch when he shall recognize his existence as that of Jehovah." It is fitting that, divesting man of the denominations of human time and place, Poe was able to say, "I have no desire to live since I have done *Eureka.*" In theory, Tocqueville sanctions Poe's audacious work which at least two modern poets, W. H. Auden and Paul Valéry, consider original and profound.[14]

4

The rise of democracy, Tocqueville thought, not only had an effect on conceptions of religion and cosmology, but also influenced attitudes toward the past and future. Aristocratic societies were favorable to the poetic imagination in regard to the past; democratic societies were more interested in the future.

Depending in part on men's sense of history for approval, "Aristocracy naturally leads the human mind to the contemplation of the past and fixes it there. Democracy, on the contrary, gives men a sort of instinctive distaste for what is ancient.... Among a democratic people poetry will not be fed with legends or the memorials of old traditions" (2:76). Hawthorne's use of New England legends and history has made it natural for scholars to speak of his search for American subjects and to cope with him as an American writer. There has been also some attempt to show that Poe used southern folklore and that the region's fondness for ghost stories and tales of people buried alive conditioned Poe's interests in the macabre, but there is little evidence that either southern or national history directly intruded in his poems and stories. While Emerson was writing a Concord memorial hymn, a poem on Daniel Webster, or even "Hamatreya," with its background of Concord history for retelling a passage from the *Vishnu Purana*, Poe was not writing poems on the battle of Yorktown, or Patrick Henry, George Washington, and John Marshall.

Yet Poe himself was enthusiastic about American history. Reviewing J. K. Paulding's *Life of Washington*, Poe read the biography "with a degree of interest seldom excited ... by the perusal of any book whatever" (H 9:13). He had earlier observed that such a biography "succinct in form, yet in a matter sufficiently comprehensive, has long been a desideratum" when he commented on a life of Washington written in Latin prose by Francis Glass. Speaking of the author as a man he "reverenced and loved," Poe (teasingly or mockingly) concluded: "Were we not Alexander, we should have luxuriated in being Glass" (H 8:102-4). Of Joseph Story's "Discourse on Chief Justice Marshall" and Horace Binney's "Eulogy" to Marshall, Poe said he had read them "with an interest *created* by long admiration for the subject" (H 8:114-15). He also defended George Bancroft, whose history was written to glorify American democracy. Poe objected that critics who wished to damn Bancroft's work praised his style, as if to say the matter was hardly worth notice. Poe, however, approved of the work as "philosophical history," and commended the author "because no amount of philosophy has yet taught him to despise a minute accuracy in point of fact" (H 14:180).

Responding to the nation's history, Poe was nevertheless critical when

William Gilmore Simms attempted to use it in fiction. The objection is clear in a review of Simms's *The Partisan* (1835). Simms had advertised that the novel was originally intended to be one of a series devoted to the War of Independence, but also had said that he did not know whether he would continue the series. "Upon the whole," Poe wrote, "we think that he had better not. . . ." He based the advice on the view that the interweaving of historical fact with fiction is at all times hazardous. Simms, Poe felt, had failed in confining either the truth or the fable within its legitimate domain. Poe approved of the novelist's depiction of the conduct of General Horatio Gates in South Carolina, although Simms, worried that he could not idealize Gates, found it necessary to plead the reader's favor. Having attributed gross negligence, obstinacy, and self-conceit to Gates, Simms was sustained by the best historians of the day and historical fact, Poe pointed out. "No apology is needed for stating the truth. In regard to the 'propriety of insisting upon the faults and foibles of man conspicuous in our history,' . . . it is precisely because the man *is* conspicuous in our history, that we should have no hesitation in condemning his errors" (H 8:145–47). Perhaps Poe's discriminations are related to the development of history as a science; but his criticism of the use of American history in a work of literature and his deliberate exclusion of that history belong to the configuration of attitudes Tocqueville associates with being a writer in a democracy.

Tocqueville thought, furthermore, that democratic nations, caring "little for what has been, are haunted by visions of what will be; in this direction their unbounded imagination grows and dilates beyond all measure." Here was "the widest range open" to the poets because it allowed them to remove their performances to a sufficient distance from the eye. "Democracy, which shuts the past against the poet, opens the future before him" (2:78).

When Tocqueville wrote this, Poe had already discovered that readers thrilled to imaginary stories of trips to the moon, a possibility which equally excited his poetic and scientific interest. The story of the adventures of "Hans Phaall" preceded by three weeks an account of "Lunar Discoveries," written as a hoax by Richard Locke for the New York *Sun*, a paper whose fortune was, in part, made by the interest Locke created. Nearly ten years later, in 1844, the *Sun* published another hoax, Poe's famous story of the Victoria, a balloon in which a group of men had crossed the Atlantic in seventy-five hours. For this story, which created such a sensation that the *Sun* office was surrounded by a great crowd and the edition of the paper sold for fifty cents a copy, Poe has often been derided as a low jokester, feeling superior to the poor fools he duped. Poe, reprinting "The Balloon-Hoax" as a "jeu d'esprit" thereafter, commented that "if (as some assert) the *Victoria* did not absolutely accomplish the voyage recorded it will be difficult to assign a reason why she *should* not have accomplished it" (H 5:224). Poe also used a balloon voyage – aboard the *Skylark*, April 1, 1848 – as a pretext for a satiric view of American life in "Mellonta Tauta," which was published in 1849. Without sharing the belief in progress and indefinite perfectibility to which many Americans subscribed, he nevertheless enjoyed contemplating possible future achievements. In "The Power of Words" (1845) Agathos argues that the mathematicians, through the agency of algebraic analysis, saw "that this species of analysis itself, had within itself a capacity for indefinite progress" and "that there were no bounds conceivable to its advancement and applicability, except within the intellect of him who advanced or applied it" (H 6:142). Students of Poe have even suggested that he forecast radio waves in "The Power of Words."[15] He also speculated about the nature of existence after the apocalyptic end of the earth described in "The Conversation of Eiros and Charmion" (1839). But more importantly, as Valéry pointed out, Poe "offered the first and most striking example of the scientific tale" as well as "the modern cosmogonic poem. . . ."[16] These efforts were stimulated by a radically restless imagination in a new world. "I live continually in a reverie of the future," Poe wrote to James Russell Lowell in 1844. ". . . I have been too deeply conscious of the mutability and evanescence of temporal things, to give any continuous effort to anything – to be consistent in anything. My life has been *whim* – impulse – passion – a longing for solitude – a scorn of all things present, in an earnest desire for the future" (O: 2:257).

5

A democratic people's interest in the future may be favorable to the imaginative powers of the poet, but in Tocqueville's view the democratic society itself is hardly more favorable for the writer who would idealize the present than for one who wished to draw upon history. "After having deprived poetry of the past," Tocqueville argued, "the principle of equality robs it in part of the present" (2:78).

The language, dress, and daily actions of men were not, Tocqueville assumed, poetic in themselves; "and, if it were otherwise, it would cease to be so, because they are too familiar to all those whom the poet would speak of them" (2:80) in a democratic society. Tocqueville explained that among aristocratic nations

there is a certain number of privileged personages whose situation is, as it were, without and above the condition of man; to these, power, wealth, fame, wit, refinement, and distinction in all things appear to belong. The crowd never sees them very closely or·does not watch them in minute details, and little is needed to make the descriptions of such men poetical. [2:76]

On the other hand, he observed, there are in the same society, "classes so ignorant, low and enslaved that they are no less fit objects for poetry, from the excess of their rudeness and wretchedness, than the former are from their greatness and refinement." Because the different classes in an aristocratic community are widely separated and imperfectly acquainted with each other, there is again more possibility for idealizing such persons in literature: "The imagination may always represent them with some addition to, or some subtraction from, what they really are." Democracy, however, "reduced each individual to smaller and better known proportions." In democratic communities "men are all insignificant and very much alike," each man "instantly sees all his fellows when he surveys himself," and this "general similitude" of individuals lessens the likelihood of an idealization of men and achievements. The "poets of democratic ages, therefore, can never take any man in particular as the subject of the piece" (2:77). Such developments would precipitate the death of tragedy and the disappearance of the tragic hero as they were traditionally conceived, although neither Tocqueville nor Poe observed that inevitable result.

Discussing the relationship between verse satire and class formations, Poe debated with himself in a way that points up the interest he had in questions Tocqueville raised. "An ingenuous friend at our elbow," Poe wrote in 1845, had suggested that in England "satire abounds, because the people find a proper target in the aristocracy, whom they (the people) regard as a distant race of beings, with whom they have nothing in common. . . ." For that reason, they relish "even the most virulent abuse of the upper classes with a gusto undiminished by any feeling that they (the poeple) have a personal concern in it." In America, the friend at the elbow continued, "the people who write are the people who read — and thus in satirizing the people we satirize ourselves, and can feel no real sympathy in the satire." Poe, however, found "all this . . . more verisimilar than true. Our friend forgets that no individual ever considers himself as one of the mass. He, the individual, is the pivot — the immovable and central pivot, on which all the rest of the world spins round." Poe concluded, therefore, that "we may abuse people by wholesale and with a perfectly clear conscience, so far as regards any compunction for offending one single human being of the whole multitude of which that people is

composed." He thought Americans suffered from the "sin of imitation —
a sin perpetrated by all colonies upon the mother countries from which
they spring" and were content "with doing what not only has been done
before, but what (however well done) had been done *ad nauseam*." He saw
"no need of transcendental reasons to account for it" (H 12:107-9).

With or without transcendental reasons, Poe himself had written a
light satirical piece, "The Devil in the Belfry" (1839), about the Dutch
borough of Vondervotteimittiss where the buildings were precisely alike
inside and out; the boys and men dressed alike; all citizens had the same
preoccupations with their cabbages and clocks, and echoed one another
when they spoke. Poe's homespun details are as clear and colorful as a
genre painting of a domestic scene, but life is characterized by close con-
formities disrupted and turned into an uproar by "a very diminutive
foreign-looking young man," a wag who was taken by the burghers to be
"old Nick himself." It was easy, then, to abuse people "by wholesale."

Despite Poe's judgment of the views of a "friend" whose analysis
sounds as if he had been reading Tocqueville, the attention Poe gives to
the realities of the American literary situation and to the aims of the
satirist in a democratic context is salient. The drolleries of "The Devil
in the Belfry" express Poe's consciousness of the limits of provincial
homogeneous communities "with but a trifling variety of pattern." The
artisans, "the carvers of Vondervotteimittiss[,] have never been able to
carve more than two objects — a time-piece and a cabbage. But these
they do exceedingly well, and intersperse them, with singular ingenuity,
wherever they find room for the chisel." One would like to think that
Poe was ridiculing himself as well as the good Dutch burghers, but ironist
that he sometimes was, he seems to have had little self-irony. Perhaps he
could not afford it. One has, by contrast, the self-irony in that other
biographer of the soul, E. A. Robinson, whose attractive modesty endears
him to us as Poe has never endeared himself to us. Poe's singular ingenuities exist, however, in relation to cultural phenomena which are as distinct
from the "transcendental" as his pronouncement would have us believe.

Poe's disregard for his own time as a historical period in setting the
events of his poems and tales was long a critical commonplace. The phrase
"out of Time" in his poem "Dream-Land" has been applied to much of
his work as if that were all there was to it. Since an aura of "timelessness"
is scarcely atypical in poetry including that by Poe, the quality can be
explained as stringent practice of a poetic principle. "We must object,"
Poe said in a criticism of "Orion" by the English poet, R. M. Horne, "to
the personal and political allusions — the Corn Law question, for example —
to Wellington's statue, etc. These things, of course, have no business in a
poem" (H 11:266). Prose fiction, nonetheless, is supposed to show more

respect for such realities. The theory of "the fact in fiction," as Mary McCarthy put it, [17] insists on firm dates, for instance. In some of Poe's stories, such as "The Tell-Tale Heart," the events seem suspended in historical time. The opening of "Metzengerstein" reads: "Horror and fatality have been stalking abroad in all ages. Why then give a date to this story I have to tell?" The point is hardly uncharacteristic of other tales. In still others Poe uses the convention of the half-specific "18—" for dating events: "during the spring and part of the summer of 18—" ("The Murders in the Rue Morgue"); "It was on the tenth day of July, 18—" ("A Descent into the Maelström"); and "during the autumn of 18—" ("The System of Dr. Tarr and Prof. Fether"). The events of a few of the stories are carefully dated, although the stories do not necessarily give the illusion of a specific period: "during the chivalrous reign of the third Edward" ("King Pest"); "The French army had entered Toledo. The Inquisition was in the hands of its enemies" ("The Pit and the Pendulum"); "during the fall of the year 1827" ("A Tale of the Ragged Mountain"); "My namesake was born on the nineteenth of January, 1813 . . . the day of my own nativity" ("William Wilson"); and "upon my return to the United States a few months ago" (in the preface, dated July 1838 for *Arthur Gordon Pym*). When Hans Phaall says "on the ------ day of -----, (I am not positive about the date)," or the narrator of "Ligeia" says "I cannot, for my soul, remember . . . when . . . I first became acquainted with the lady, . . . " literary principles, or if one prefers, "tricks of the trade," are operative just as they are in all the instances cited. The delineation of the ideal required considerable ingenuity if one were a writer in a democratic society: "the indispensable history," "the wind and weather of daily life"[18] were missing.

What resources were there for writing about human beings in a society that conceptually if not in practice denied the strict old class distinctions? Poe has been stereotyped as a writer who preferred mad aristocrats living in Gothic splendor without and above the grubby conditions of egalitarian mortals. "Metzengerstein" (1832), depicting the fatal rivalry between two "illustrious houses" — that of the powerful Baron Metzengerstein and that of Count Berlifitzing, "less ancient and less wealthy . . . although loftily descended" — is supposed to set the pattern for Poe's nightmare sympathies. In "The Cask of Amontillado" (1846) the "Montresors . . . were a great and numerous family," but Fortunato, "rich, respected, admired," forgets the anti-Masonic Montresor's "arms." In between the early Metzengerstein and the late Fortunato are a panoply of "privileged" subjects: the figures of "The Assignation" (1834), "Berenice" (1835), "Ligeia" (1838), "The Fall of the House of Usher" and "William Wilson" (1839), "The Masque of the Red Death" and "The Oval Portrait" (1842), as well as C. Auguste Dupin, "of an excellent, indeed an illustrious family," who is reduced to the recreations of a detective at the expense of the police in the three tales of ratiocination (1840, 1842, and 1845). It is not possible to match story for story, but there are also the bellows mender who is the hero of "Hans Phaall" (1835); the son of "a respectable trader in sea-stores at Nantucket and grandson of "an attorney in good practice" who "had speculated successfully in stocks of the Edgarton New Bank," the son of a sea-captain, and a line-manager who was the son of an Indian squaw[19] and a fur-trader, the principals in *Arthur Gordon Pym* (1837-38); the criminal who wears a "second-handed *roquelaire*" under which is glimpsed a diamond and a dagger in "The Man of the Crowd" (1840); the three fishermen of "A Descent into the Maelström" (1841); the classless young murderer of "The Tell-Tale Heart" (1843); the poor alcoholic of "The Black Cat" (1843); and the dwarfed court jester of "Hop-Frog" (1849). Such a pedestrian list is beside the point except in so far as it counters the stereotype that Poe's work is an escape from life by dreams of wit and refinement, distinctions of privilege and social status. "Wit"? It is almost non-existent in the house of Usher or "The Tell-Tale Heart." Ingenuity or madness, intelligence or criminality, is not limited to any stratum of society but must count as dramatic differences among people.

Poe, the writer who lived by assessing readers' attitudes, and the critic who worked at defining literary principles, was interested in what he called "the trying subject of *caste*" (H 15:85). Soliciting support for editorial projects, he spoke of needing "caste," which he suggested that as a stranger in circles other than those of fellow writers he did not have (O 1:154, 2:152). In a review of Harry Lorrequer's *Charles O'Malley: The Irish Dragoon*, Poe criticized the author for a "blind and grovelling worship of mere rank" (H 11:94). Commenting on Catherine M. Sedgewick's *The Linwoods*, he said it was "the old story of the meek and trusting spirit bowed down to the dust by falsehood of a deceiver, . . . Jasper Meredith, an accomplished and aristocratical coxcomb," but Poe praised the writer for "a striking picture" of Mrs. Meredith, "the heartless and selfish woman of fashion and aristocracy" (H 7:97). He wrote of a sentimental play, "The Honeymoon," that it had little to recommend it and objected that a "duke (Aranza) wedding, in his character of duke, a haughty gentlewoman (Juliana) makes her believe after marriage, that he is not only a peasant, but more brutal and disgusting than peasant ever yet was" (H 12:189).

In retrospect, it is amusing to note Poe's awareness of the American reader's need to be prepared for a new type of hero, a "common man." Giving the title of a novel to be reviewed, *Horse-Shoe Robinson* (1835), John P. Kennedy's revolutionary war story, Poe followed with a parenthetical charge: "Be not alarmed at the title, gentle reader!"[20] Then, as if to snare the gentle reader's curiosity, Poe wrote:

> The principal character in the novel, upon whom the chief interest of the story turns, and who, in accordance with the right usage of novel writing, should be considered the hero, and should have given a title to the book, is Brevet Major Arthur Butler of the continental army. . . . But Mr. K has ventured, at his own peril, to set at defiance the common idea of propriety in this important matter, and, not having the fear of the critic before his eyes, has thought it better to call his work by the name of a very singular personage, whom all readers will agree in pronouncing worthy of the honor thus conferred him.

Poe explained that Horse-Shoe Robinson's nickname was derived from the facts that he was a blacksmith and lived in a nook of land hemmed in by a semicircular bend of water. He was, for Poe, fully entitled to "the character of 'an original' . . . the life and soul of the drama — the bone and sinew of the book — its very breath — its every thing which gives it strength and vitality." Poe stated that he entered at once into the spirit and meaning of the author (H 7:4-8). If it is objected that Kennedy was the patron and friend of Poe, he was consistent in judgment when he turned to other writers. Longfellow's "The Village Blacksmith" had for Poe "the beauty of simple-mindedness as a genuine thesis . . . inimitably handled until the concluding stanza, where the spirit of legitimate poesy is aggrieved in the deduction of a moral . . ." (H 11:77). Reviewing Simms's *The Partisan,* Poe considered Major Robert Singleton, a character rather similar to Kennedy's Major Butler, "a non-entity." Of Simms's revolutionary war hero, Poe said that Singleton was a "tall, well-made youth," with a steed which the reader might take for granted was quite as tall and equally well made. "The hand of Miss Katherine is, as a matter of course, the reward of the Major's gallantry" (H 7:148-50). Poe thought that Cooper's typical subject, "the love of Maude Meredith for Robert Willoughby [,] is painted with exquisite skill and truth," but Poe did not appreciate Cooper's idealized aristocrat. Willoughby "is a nobody; that is to say, there is nothing about him which may be looked upon as distinctive. Perhaps he is rather silly than otherwise . . . he is too often on stilts. . . ." But the critical Poe could not, he said, be enthusiastic enough about the Indian, Wyandotté, who gives the title to the Cooper novel in which Willoughby figures: "The Indian . . . is the great feature of the book . . . . Indeed, we think this 'forest gentleman' superior to the other noted heroes of his kind — the heroes which have been immortalized by our novelist" (H 11:213). Poe was also receptive to the work of Carolina M.

Kirkland, the first of a series of writers to take the agricultural West (then including southern Michigan) as a subject during the period after Cooper's *The Prairie* (1827). He noted that Mrs. Kirkland's first book, *A New Home – Who'll Follow?* (1839), wrought an undoubted sensation, not so much because of picturesque description, racy humor, or animated individual portraiture, but because of its truth and novelty. He observed:

> The west at the time was a field comparatively untrodden by the sketcher or the novelist. In certain works, to be sure, we had obtained brief glimpses of characters strange to us sojourners in the civilized east, but to Mrs. Kirkland alone we were indebted for acquaintance with the *home* and home-life of the backwoodsman. . . . She has placed before us the veritable settlers of the forest, with all their peculiarities, national and individual; their free and fearless spirit; their homely utilitarian views; their shrewd outlooking for self-interest; their thrifty care and inventions multiform; their coarseness of manner, united with real delicacy and substantial kindness when their sympathies are called into action – in a word, with all the characteristic of the Yankee, in a region where the salient points of character are unsmoothed by contact with society. [H 15:85-86]

Poe's criticism, then, ranged through the American subjects of his contemporaries, cut down the clichés of caste, and consciously aided the transition from an aristocratic to a new literature. Cultural historians calling the period that begins with Poe "the American Literary Renaissance" betrayed the slow, painful development of a literature which was not the revival of a tradition because there was not one to revive. Poe was almost obsessed with being an original writer. And when Whitman announced, in 1855, "Here comes one among the well-beloved stone cutters and plans with decision and science and sees the solid and beautiful forms of the future where there are now no solid forms," he knew whereof he spoke. Poe was at least chronologically one of Whitman's predecessors who knew that American literature was precariously beginning.

It is not only in the criticism that Poe reflects the dynamics of the American experiment for the writer. For the first of the published poems, *Tamerlane*, Poe made an accepted choice. Consciously aiming to idealize Tamerlane, he said it "was more than probable" that the hero was descended from the family of Genghis Khan, but was "vulgarly supposed to have been the son of a shepherd, and to have raised himself to the throne by his own address" (M 26). The young writer explained that he had taken "the full liberty of a poet" and followed the vulgar notion: Tamerlane was a cottager and a peasant who became "great." Tamerlane says that he was "Uncheck'd by sarcasm, and scorn/ Of those, who hardly will conceive/ That any should become great, born/ In their own sphere —[.] " Poe added another footnote: "Although Tamerlane speaks this, it is not the less true" (M 34). Only eighteen at the time of the poem's publication, Poe was not simply writing about himself. He commented on Tamerlane's attitude:

> It is a matter of the greatest difficulty to make the generality of mankind believe that one, with whom they are upon terms of intimacy, should be called, in the world, a "great man." The reason is evident. There are few great men. Their actions are consequently viewed by the mass of people thro' the medium of distance. — The prominent parts of their character are alone noted; and those properties, which are minute and common to everyone, not being observed, seem to have no connection with a great character. [M 34-35]

The tensions could hardly be more American: the belief that the individual could "raise himself" by his own efforts, and the difficulty to idealize the great who are seen to have characteristics in common with everyone else. Poe's footnote concluded: "Who ever reads the private memorials, correspondence, etc., which have become so common in our time without wondering that 'great men' should act and think 'so abominably'?" Tamerlane's speech, having been interrupted by the footnote, continues with a reference to those who

> will not believe
> That they shall stoop in life to one
> Whom daily they are wont to see
> Familiarly — whom Fortune's sun
> Hath ne'er shone dazzlingly upon
> Lowly — and of their own degree. . . .

In the early days of the republic, it can be noted, Virginians had among them more than their share of great men — men of their own degree. Whitman would write in "Song of Myself" (1855): "Have you outstript the rest? are you the President?/ It is a trifle. . . ." A democratic spirit has its strict ironies.

The "trying" assumptions about "caste" occasionally arose with respect to Poe's fiction. The first long tale is uncertain in tone, half farcical and half serious in its account of the adventures of a bellows mender. An alteration of the title may reflect nothing more than that uncertainty, but even though Poe's original as well as final title was "Hans Phaall," the tale was first reprinted without authorization as "Lunar Discoveries,

Extraordinary Aerial Voyage by Baron Hans Phaall" in a New York paper in 1835 (Quinn and O'Neill, 2:1075). Hans Phaall, a bellows mender? Not even Benjamin Franklin could have assured a willing suspension of disbelief for that hoax. It needed a baron. The Norwegian fisherman who tells of surviving a maelström is one of Poe's ratiocinative minds. Observing a barrel in the whirling waters of the sea, the fisherman was able to analyze the principle of the cylinder's resistance to the suction of the vortex and to ride the cask out in "A Descent into the Maelström." Often discussed by critics as one of Poe's metaphors of the psychological abyss, the story has never been considered one in which Poe glorified "the common man," yet it was criticized by a French journalist-translator, E. D. Forgues, in 1846 because the "paysan" could not have thought out the theory which saved him.[21] For Poe's generation it was, after all, a long time (1885) before Mark Twain would grow Huck Finn wild from the heartland, and it was another decade or two before a shirtsleeve democrat would find an original form for the problematic, loose verbalizations of a democratic ideology.

In Poe's work there are only traces of the idealization of the individual of slender importance. Hardly a leitmotif, certainly not a political issue, there is in Poe's early (1832) story of the Castle Metzengerstein "an insignificant and misshapen little page, . . . whose opinions were of the least possible importance," but he alone "had the effrontery" to perceive correctly the fearful relationship between the Baron and the rival soul embodied in the horse that triumphed over the Baron. Poe was always on the side of effrontery. Among the many variables in considering the audacities, there is a straight line from that "insignificant little page" to one of the last stories, "Hop-Frog: or, the Eight Chained Ourang-Outangs" (1849). "I am not able to say with precision," the narrator remarks, "from what country Hop-Frog originally came. It was from some barbarous region, however, that no person ever heard of − a vast distance from the court of our king." Hop-Frog's value as the court's professional fool was trebled by the fact that he was a dwarf and a cripple. He "could only get along by a sort of interjectional gait − something between a leap and a wriggle − a movement that afforded illimitable amusement, and of course consolation, to the king. . . ." The king troubled himself very little about "the refinements, or, as he called them, the 'ghosts' of wit. . . . Over-niceties wearied him." Practical jokes suited his taste. The story, then, is centered on the conflict between a tyrannical arbiter of taste and the taunted, insulted fool hired to entertain him. The cost is high. The king knew that "Hop-Frog was not fond of wine; for it excited the poor cripple almost to madness; and madness is no comfortable feeling." But the king "took pleasure in forcing Hop-Frog to drink and (as the king called it) 'to be merry.' " In observance of a grand occasion, he determined to have a masquerade and nothing could be done without the assistance of Hop-Frog, who was resourceful in the way of getting up pageants, and arranging costumes: " 'Come here, Hop-Frog, ... let us have the benefit of your invention. We want characters — *characters* — man — something novel — out of the way. We are wearied with this everlasting sameness. Come, drink! the wine will brighten your wits.' " Hop-Frog's wits were so brightened and bewildered that he turned a masquerade into a maniacal last jest in which the king and seven great ministers were tarred, plastered with flax — to look like orangoutans — and burned alive. The fool's calculated savagery, proposed as "a capital diversion — one of my own country frolics," turns the pathos of the individual of slender means into brutalizing rage that does not recommend either the society or its imaginative man.

The lack of "real" characters, the poor sense of "real human beings," the preference for unidentified or anonymous narrators (sometimes witnesses and sometimes perpetrators) of terrible events, the failure to take "any man in particular as the subject of a piece" — all of these monotonies in the work of Poe are to the point. In the light of this typology, the nameless king's request in the story of Hop-Frog is summarily ironic. The king seems to have anticipated the critics' view of Poe's "characters" as shadows of each other or variations of the author's macabre self. Poe, writing about the difference between short story and novel, defended the limitations of the form for which he had stringent principles: "In the tale proper — where there is no space for development of character or for great profusion and variety of incident — mere construction is, of course, far more imperatively demanded . . ." (H 16:171). It is generally agreed that Poe's major achievement is the development of the tale. The fact of the matter is that Poe was both a little man and a genius in his own time. He had the effrontery to seize the imagination of a country in which the taste for quick, strong, crude emotions had to be appeased and the desire for a superior native literature had to be reconciled with that taste.

From a different, outraged perspective, William Carlos Williams's poem "To Elsie" (1923) speaks of themes and situations manifest or implicit in the work of Poe. "The pure products of America," Williams charges, "go crazy —/ mountain folk from Kentucky/ or the ribbed north end of/ Jersey/ with its isolate lakes and / valleys. . . ." Williams then describes the relationship between

> devil-may-care men who have taken
> to railroading

> out of sheer lust of adventure —
> and young slatterns. . .
>
> tricked out . . .
> with gauds
> from imaginations which have no
>
> peasant traditions to give them
> character
> but flutter and flaunt
>
> sheer rags — succumbing without
> emotion
> save numbed terror
>
> . . . which they cannot express —[22]

Williams's poem is about an American imagination that Poe apprehended. The gauds he tricked out to express it are ambiguous as documents for proof of political sympathies or attitudes. As literary documents, however, they are signs of an attempt to integrate principles of an aesthetic, theories of genre, and the exigencies of the culture.

6

"I am persuaded," Tocqueville states, "that in the end democracy diverts the imagination from all that is external to man and fixes it on man alone" (2:77). When skepticism had depopulated heaven and the progress of democratic ideas had reduced each individual to smaller and better-known proportions, "the poets, not yet aware of what they could substitute for the great themes that were departing together with the aristocracy, turned their eyes to inanimate nature." Setting themselves to describe streams and mountains, they originated "that kind of poetry which had been called, by way of distinction, *descriptive*." Tocqueville disagreed with those who thought "this embellished delineation of all the physical and inanimate objects which cover the earth was the kind of poetry peculiar to democratic ages." He believed it belonged "only to a period of transition" (2:77). He observed that in Europe "people talk a great deal about the wilds of America, but the Americans themselves never think about them; and they may be said not to perceive the mighty forests that surround them till they fall beneath the hatchet." American eyes, however, are fixed upon the "march across these wilds, draining swamps, turning the course of rivers, peopling solitudes, and subduing nature." This magnificent image "may be said to haunt everyone of them in his least as well as in his most important actions and to be always flitting before his mind" (2:78). Democratic nations "may amuse themselves for a while with considering the productions of nature, but they are excited in reality only by a survey of themselves" (2:77). Tocqueville thought nothing conceivable is "so petty, so insipid, so crowded with paltry interests — in one word, so anti-poetic — as the life of a man in the United States. But among the thoughts which it suggests, there is always one that is full of poetry." This thought is "the hidden nerve which gives vigour to the whole frame" (2:78-79).

The critical Poe also expressed a view rather consonant with Tocqueville's on nature poetry. In 1837 the American said of Bryant's poem "The Prairies" that its "descriptive beauty is of the highest order. The peculiar points of interest in the Prairie are vividly shown forth, and as a local painting, the work is altogether excellent" (H 9:282). Poe praised Bryant's "vivid picture of the life of a hunter in the desert," the subject of another of the prairie poems. "The poet, however, is here greatly indebted to his subject" (H 9:288). Poe's reservations are explicit in a brief final judgment about the genre. In "Fifty Suggestions" (1845) he wrote:

> Bryant and Street [a minor poet included in Griswold's anthology] are both, essentially, descriptive poets; and descriptive poetry, even in its happiest manifestation, is *not* of the highest order. But the distinction between Bryant and Street is very broad. While the former, in reproducing the sensible images of nature, reproduces the sentiments with which he regards them, the latter gives us the images and nothing more. He never forces us to feel what he must have felt. [H 14:182-83]

Poe was certainly not insensitive to the American landscape. The notion that Poe's work "lacks a . . . real nature element" is hardly accurate. Even in the early poem *Al Aaraaf* the extra-terrestrial paradise is conceived as a lovely sphere of green fields, dim plains, streams, mountains, and crags athwart the solemn sky; there is only one building on a high mountain. Nature was a part of the vital experience of Poe's life and consequently of his imagination. His appreciation and use of the experience account for some of the most subtle effects in both the poetry and prose. His idealization of the solitudes and great spaces evident in "The Lake," the dream work, the images of ancient ruins, and even the kingdom of death, depends on an intimate sense of natural phenomena. In "The Island of the Fay" the prose poem evokes the radiance of evening among the "green tombs" of nature where a gentle fay yields up life, as mankind yield up their lives, in the quickened pace of the fall of darkness. But Poe found "an excess of glory" in the constant view of the extent and grandeur of American nature. "Grandeur," Poe concluded, "startles, excites — and then fatigues, depresses" (H 6:189-90). In one of the last poems, "Eldorado," the interest is not in what Marianne Moore once called embarrassingly direct description; we find instead a lighthearted, calm acceptance of a lonely terrain and a dramatization of a bold rider through the reaches of time and space. Except as the sense of a journey in time suggests it, the sense of space is almost taken for granted.

The young Poe's American eyes were wide open to the sources of poetry Tocqueville thought at hand for the taking. Sharing what he believed a universal enthusiasm for works devoted to the exploits of the type Tocqueville also found evocative to the democratic imagination, Poe reviewed Theodore Irving's *Conquest of Florida* in 1835. Without the benefit of Tocqueville, Poe wrote: "There is so much of romance in the details of Spanish conquests in America, that a history of any one of the numerous expeditions for discovery and conquest, possesses the charm of the most elaborate fiction, even while it bears the marks of general truth" (H 8:37). Poe almost anticipates Tocqueville's analysis:

> There are in the histories of their [the Spaniards'] exploits, so many displays of dauntless courage — of skill in overcoming difficulties — of the power of a few disciplined warriors, to contend successfully with hosts of equally brave, but untutored savages — and so many exhibitions of the generous qualities of the soldier, that in the glare of brilliant achievement, and the excitement of thrilling incident, we are tempted to overlook the injustices and cruelty which marked the footsteps of the conquerors. [H 8:38]

Poe's imagination was not dazzled, he asserted, "with descriptions of boundless wealth and regal magnificence — although the chiefs are not decked in 'barbaric pearls and gold' — [but] their sturdy resistance, and the varied vicissitudes created by the obstacles which nature presented to the conqueror's march, afford numberless details of great interest" (H 8:39).

Poe was equally responsive to James Hall's *Sketches of History, Life and Manners in the West*, for which he wrote a notice in 1835. The book treated such subjects as the policy of the government in regard to the Indians, the adventures of the white settlers on the Ohio, the difficulties experienced in Mississippi navigation, and various military operations carried on in the wilderness of the Northwest (an appendix included some previously unpublished papers relative to the first settlement of Kansas). "Wild romance and exciting adventure," Poe said, "form its staple" (H 8:108-9).

Poe wrote one of the longest reviews he ever published when Washington Irving's *Astoria: or, Anecdotes of an Enterprise beyond the Rocky Mountains* appeared in 1836. Poe praised the story of John Jacob Astor's project to extend the fur trade with the Indians in all the western and northwestern regions of North America. The adjectives he used to describe Astor were "high minded," "indomitable," "an aspiring spirit," "a genius bold, fertile and expansive." Of course, some of these were quoted from Irving who was, in Poe's words, "alive to the exciting interest of the subject." By speaking of the motives which actuated Astor in an enterprise so extensive, Irving had done Astor simplest justice, Poe believed. Astor was already wealthy beyond the ordinary desires of man, "but now he aspired to that honorable fame which is awarded to men of similar scope of mind, who by their great commercial enterprises, have enriched nations, peopled wildernesses, and extended the bounds of empire" (H 9:207-43).

The early Poe reviews showed more than cursory interest in frontier experience. He noted that the "conquest" of Florida was "an ill-starred expedition." Hall's account of the settlements of the West was less discouraging, and Poe found it a fund of both information and amusement. But, while the courageous Astor ironically stayed home and did what he could to save the Astoria enterprise, it failed; the forgotten men he sent out on the "vast series of adventures" suffered, in the words of Poe, every extremity of fatigue, hunger, thirst, anxiety, terror, and despair.

By 1843 Poe expressed disenchantment with the attention to native exploits. He wrote of Cooper's *Wynadotté* that "the forest subject" gave assurance the story was a good one; Cooper, Poe said, had never been known to fail, either in the forest or on the sea. "The interest," he stated, "has no reference to plot . . . but depends upon the nature of the theme. . . ." Poe explained: "This theme – life in the wilderness – is one of intrinsic and universal interest, appealing to the heart of man in all phases; a theme, like that of life upon the ocean, so unfailingly omniprevalent in its power of arresting attention" could hardly fail to succeed. (Poe himself had published *The Narrative of Arthur Gordon Pym of Nantucket* in 1837-38.) He concluded, however, that such themes were being handled "ad nauseam" through "the instinctive perception of the universal interest which appertains to them" (H 11:205-6).

Poe's forte as a writer was not the depiction of the "march across" the wilds and the efforts to subdue nature. He thought nature was more powerful than the transient and mortal human being; he found very early that readers responded to that view. His first literary success came when he submitted six stories and a poem to a contest conducted by the *Baltimore Saturday Visiter* in the fall of 1833. The judges, John P.

Kennedy, Esq., John H. B. Latrobe, Esq., and Dr. J. H. Miller, gave the poor and unknown Poe the larger of the two prizes, fifty dollars, for a story, "MS. Found in a Bottle." The hero of the story is a man ill-used in his own country, estranged from his family and his heritage, but also a person of exceptional education, predisposed toward the rational and scientific view of phenomena, restless and nervous. He takes a sea journey. The violent changes in the physical world induce unrelievable psychological states. In an initial tempest only two men on board ship survive. They endure the swelling of black stupendous seas where at times they "gasped for breath at an elevation beyond the albatross — at times became dizzy with the velocity of . . . the ship's descent into some watery hell, where the air grew stagnant and no sound disturbed the slumbers of the kraken." Later the ship is struck by another ten times larger, and the hero, hurled onto the rigging of the larger ship, is the only survivor. The larger ship is of a kind he cannot identify from his knowledge of ships: "What she *is not*, I can easily perceive; what she *is*, I fear it is impossible to say." Possessed of a feeling which admits of no analysis and for which the past has not prepared him, he wonders whether futurity itself will offer a key.

Americans were, no doubt, fully alive to the magnificent images of themselves which Tocqueville remarked; Poe, from whatever sources, provided a metaphor for the experience of a man in a strange world that must have spoken to the American readers' experience which did not always culminate in good fortune and optimism. One wonders if the ambivalent responses to Poe as man and writer are not rooted in the fact that he expressed what Americans have historically known: the dark, overpowering greatness of a place and a society not quite like the known places and societies of the past; the individual's sense of inadequacy as a survivor of physical danger and emotional stress in a world beyond tradition — the new world; and, finally, the consequent need for hidden nerve. When the estranged hero of Poe's prize-winning story finds himself on board the unknown ship, he spends much effort avoiding discovery, but then at last he gets courage enough to show himself only to find that nobody sees him.

Hidden nerve? Poe specialized in it as if it were endemic. It is central to *The Adventures of Arthur Gordon Pym*, to the detective stories, to the balloon hoax and "The Gold-Bug." ("What ho!" the amusing epigraph of Legrand's story about the secret and anxious search for buried treasure reads, "this fellow is dancing mad! He has been bitten by a Tarantula.") Henry James's notorious pronouncement that "an enthusiasm for Poe is the mark of a decidedly primitive stage of reflection" placed the earlier writer at the barbarous beginning of American culture. The comment, nevertheless, was directed as much toward Baudelaire as toward Poe. In ⸴

The Golden Bowl James says of the European prince that he "remembered to have read as a boy a wonderful tale by Allan Poe . . .which was a thing to show, by the way, what imagination Americans *could* have: the story of the shipwrecked Gordon Pym" (p. 22). "Hidden nerve" is a theme for juveniles.

There is, however, another, less commendable kind of hidden nerve, about which Tocqueville was probably not speaking, but about which Poe was an authority. A character secretly schemes to ensnare an unsuspecting enemy, one who has wronged the character and must be made to suffer and die: the raw theme is decidedly one for adults. In "The Cask of Amontillado" (1846) and "Hop-Frog," both testimonies of hate, Poe reveals unflinchingly that the hidden nerve of the privileged but insulted Montresor is brutal cowardice, and the hidden nerve of the deprived, frustrated, and insulted "Hop-Frog" turns him into a daring but fang-toothed, raging mad dog. In the *Marginalia,* December 1846, Poe commented as if to justify the morally reprehensible, ruthless Montresor: "That man is not truly brave who is afraid either to seem or to be, when it suits him, a coward" (H 16:119). There is hardly any justification for the cool, treacherous Montresor. And though a critic or two will defend "Hop-Frog," for whose behavior Poe carefully and sympathetically accounts, the description of his terrible rage as he takes his revenge on the great king and the sycophantic ministers seems to be the author's final word on the cost of "hidden" nerve. No heroes here. Then Poe, in "Eldorado" (1849), charges a gallant knight grown old and weak to ride boldly, ride boldly "Over the Mountains/ Of the Moon" and "Down the Valley of the Shadow," but the simplicities of the metaphor did not sustain Poe and they have not sustained the American imagination. Discrepancies between the hard realities and the ideals of a democratic society diminish man's greatness. Poe, more than any other literary figure, symbolizes that diminution. The sadistic king in the story of "Hop-Frog" is delighted when the dwarfed jester proposes to terrify and astonish the company he must entertain: "Oh, this is exquisite!" exclaimed the king. "Hop-Frog! I will make a man of you." Democracy, Tocqueville said, fixes the imagination on man alone.

Poets living in democratic times, Tocqueville foresaw, "will prefer the delineation of passions and ideas to that of persons and achievements." The poet is forced "constantly to search below the external surface which is palpable to the senses, in order to read the inner soul. . . ." Tocqueville asserted that "nothing lends itself more to the delineation of the ideal than the scrutiny of the hidden depths in the immaterial nature of man." Then Tocqueville wrote as if he were a poet himself:

> I need not traverse earth and sky to discover a wondrous object woven of contrasts, of infinite greatness and littleness, of intense gloom and amazing brightness, capable at once of exciting pity, admiration, terror, contempt. I have only to look at myself. Man springs out of nothing, crosses time, and disappears forever in the bosom of God; he is seen but for a moment, wandering on the verse of the two abysses, and there he is lost. (2:80)

Poe could well have envied the prose; Tocqueville, however, passionately argued for the cause of letters:

> If man were wholly ignorant of himself, he would have no poetry in him. . . . If man clearly discerned his own nature, his imagination would remain idle and would have nothing to add to the picture. But the nature of man is sufficiently disclosed for him to know something of himself, and sufficiently obscure for all the rest to be plunged in thick darkness, in which he gropes forever, and forever in vain, to lay hold on some completer notion of his being. [2:80]

Whatever resources fail the poet in a democratic society, "Man remains, and the poet needs no more." Tocqueville then concluded: "The destinies of mankind, man himself taken aloof from his country and his age and standing in the presence of Nature and of God, with his passions, his doubts, his rare prosperities and inconceivable wretchedness, will become the chief, if not the sole, theme of poetry" among democratic nations. The greatest European poets of the new age had not, in Tocqueville's opinion, sought "to record the actions of an individual, but to throw light on some of the obscurer recesses of the human heart." There was hope, then, for the poems of democracy. "The principle of equality does not . . . destroy all the subjects of poetry: it renders them less numerous, but more vast" (2:81).

Although there is no direct evidence that Poe was familiar with Tocqueville and no allusion to the latter's work in any of the American's critical notes, it is singular that the two of them — sharing conceptions about principles and application of them to literary developments in democratic societies — stand together as recognized figures of transatlantic influence: Poe on French poetry, and Tocqueville on subsequent studies of American culture. One can only speculate about whether or not Poe read *Democracy in America*, but can imagine that Poe, if he did, would have said, "Tocqueville — damn it — that Frenchman! He knows what it is to be a poet in a republic of letters."

Poe could have been pardoned for thinking of himself and of what he wrote in the air of democracy. There was an early fragile lyric critics were later to call a juvenile imitation of Byron; it was a symptom of what would-be-unhappy boys were made of — "Dreams" (1827). A fugitive piece, Poe called it; obviously autobiographical, critics concluded.

> Yes! tho' that long dream were of hopeless sorrow,
> 'T were better than the cold reality
> Of waking life, to him whose heart must be,
> And hath been still, upon the lovely earth,
> A chaos of deep passion, from his birth.

There was also the early dramatic monologue *Tamerlane* (1827). Poe, it has been observed, "did not follow the career" of the hero, but chose to represent "an ambitious conqueror who leaves his love and returns to find his conquests futile."[23] Tamerlane's account of himself will suffice:

> among the rabble — men,
> Lion ambition is chain'd down —
> And crouches to a keeper's hand —
> Not so in deserts where the grand —
> The wild — the terrible conspire
> With their own breath to fan his fire.

Human passions were spent in encounter with the vacuities, the gulfs, the whirlpool, the abyss, natural and metaphorical. For Melville, they were "the harborless immensities," but Poe would not live to read of them or of Ahab "damned in Paradise." Melville, arguing for appreciation of American writers himself in "Hawthorne and His Mosses" (1850), would say that the piece was "By a Virginian Spending July in Vermont." He felt, because of the disparity between the mystical spirit of beauty possessing men of noble intelligence (genius) and their personal as well as their mortal limitations, that the names of all fine authors are fictitious ones.[24]

There were the rare prosperities. "Eldorado" was one of them as was the early tribute "To Helen" (1831). Perhaps the rarest of all was a poetic account of the origin of the moon and the beauty of butterflies, "Fairy-Land" (1829) — the initial surreal images suggesting time-lapse photography, and the narration transfiguring what could have been nightmare into moments of delicacy, amused delight, and enchantment. The story "Eleonora" (1841-42), a testament of love, also shared in Poe's prosperities. "The Oval Portrait" (1842) was, however, more characteristic. It is told from the perspective of a somber and wounded traveler who searches for the secret of the expression of life itself in an admirable portrait of a smiling and lovely young woman. He finds the secret in the story of her having died while her artist-husband, "grown wild with the ardor" of painting her, had not noticed that she was dying.

There were numerous trials to express what was beneath the surface. Among the best of the poems were two interior monologues: the memories of a surf-tormented and lonely man in "To One in Paradise" (1834), and the revelation of the quiet conflicts of the woman in "The Bridal Ballad" (1838); André Gide would mistakenly credit Poe as one of the originators of the form. There was the experiment with the limitations of a single point of view — the first person narrator — in "Ligeia" (also 1838). The story was an appalling exercise in the narrator's refinement and rationalization of cruelty, but readers did not know whether to trust the deluded narrator or not. The story's philosophical issue, the nature of the will, had troubled Poe from the beginning. Ligeia's vigorous "will" did not "perfect its intention," although the narrator, her husband, admitting to a state of "sudden half-consciousness" (O 1:118), would have us believe it possible that the woman's will had triumphed over death itself. The advantage of having the narrator tell the story as if he believed it credible was that the author did not have to vouch for the reliability of the account: it could be read as a covert confession of murder[25] and an extreme state of derangement if it had to be certified. Poe also had written allegory that anticipated the symbolists, "The Haunted Palace" (1839), which he had to explain to Griswold in 1841: by palace, Poe said, he meant "to imply a mind haunted by phantoms — a disordered brain" (O 1:161). (He would make the "Dream-Land" poem [1842] so clear there would be no mistaking that the images were oneiric.) There were two stories developing conceptions that originated in common figures of speech which Poe took literally and charged with meaning: "he killed his conscience"; and "he was used up." The techniques and tones were quite different. In "William Wilson" (1839) the divided self — the amoral Wilson and the moral Wilson — was symbolized as young men in conflict; when the amoral Wilson killed the moral one, "grim conscience, the spectre in his path," he simultaneously killed himself. Readers comprehended the stern allegory that demonstrated itself without the author's needing to resort to didacticism. "The Man That Was Used Up: A Tale of the Late Bugaboo and Kickapoo Campaign" (also 1839) was, on the other hand, an amusing and neglected curiosity. It depended for its satirical point on Poe's turning a slang expression, a pun, into a surreal image of a public man. Harold Rosenberg would at least refer to him as a "mechanical man," a person put together from fabricated parts, associated "with the effects upon human beings of the new machine culture."[26] But "to use up" meant, in the nineteenth century, to attack physically or verbally.[27] Poe's man, Brevet Brigadier General John A. B. C. Smith, had a "campaign" scratch or two. He was a victim of criticism. Having been "dismembered" by abuse, Smith is literally made up of artificial parts — body, limbs, wig, whiskers, eyes, teeth, palate, even the voice, all are false — put together by the best artists in the country. A "truly fine-looking fellow," "absolutely fine-looking," the narrator insists, but with a scrutinizing eye sees that there "*was* a primness, not to say stiffness . . . a degree of measured and, if I may so express it, of rectangular precision attending every movement, which, observed in a more diminutive figure, would have had the least savor in the world of affectation, pomposity, or constraint. . . ." He was "a *remarkable* man," "indeed one of the *most* remarkable men of the age." Fit, indeed, to be president, the office for which he is campaigning. Poe was quick to see beneath masks.

The subjects were not multitudinous, but they were not paltry, either. If one only had a "philosophical lynxeye," one could still discern "through the indignity-mist of Man's life . . . the dignity of Man" (H 16:161). There was the calm, inquisitive observer's pursuit of "The Man of the Crowd" (1840), and the conclusion: "It will be in vain to follow, for I shall learn no more of him, nor of his deeds." There was a sketch on "Instinct vs Reason — A Black Cat" (also 1840) that began, "The line which demarcates the instinct of brute creation from the boasted reason of man is, beyond doubt, of the most shadowy and unsatisfactory character — a boundary line far more difficult to settle than even the North-Eastern or the Oregon." Nevertheless, there was the account of Dupin's way of listening to unsaid things, his interest in "mind reading," and analysis of the free association of ideas for the companion in the detective fiction "The Murders in the Rue Morgue" (1841). "There are," the companion wrote, "few persons who have not, at some period of their lives, amused themselves in retracing the steps by which particular conclusions of their own minds have been attained." It is difficult to tell the attentive companion from Poe who is also often identified with Dupin. "The occupation," the three of them could say in one voice with regard to self-scrutiny, "is often full of interest; and he who attempts it for the first time is astonished by the apparently illimitable distance and incoherence between the starting-point and the goal." "I have only to look at myself," Tocqueville had said. It was not quite that easy. "No man," Poe would assert in 1848, "ever will dare write," and no man "*could* . . . even if he dared" write a book laying the heart bare (H 16:128).

Poe had, however, what he termed "the faculty of identification — that dominion exercised by volition over imagination which enables the mind to lose its own in a fictitious individuality" (H 7:70). The trait especially impressed the Baltimore lawyer and inventor John H. B. Latrobe, one of the judges for the contest in which Poe's "MS Found in a

Bottle" won the prize. Latrobe wrote, in a letter of December 7, 1852, that after the 1833 contest Poe called upon him sometimes

> and entered at length into discussion of subjects on which he proposed to employ his pen. When he warmed up, he was most eloquent. He spoke, at that time, with eager action . . . as he seemed to forget the world around him, as wild fancy, logical truth, mathematical analysis and wonderful combination of facts flowed, in strange commingling, from his lips, in words choice and appropriate, as though the result of closest study. I remember being particularly struck with the power that he seemed to possess of identifying himself with whatever he was describing. He related to me all the facts of a voyage to the Moon, I think (which he proposed to put on paper), with an accuracy of minute detail, and a truthfulness as regard philosophical phenomena, which impressed you with the idea that he had himself just returned from the journey, that existed only in his imagination.[28]

Poe indentified himself so completely with morbid states of mind that the fictional projections involved a process he himself did not fully comprehend; few readers would believe, of course, that he was not writing about himself from the time he began with the heuristic story of the obsessive Egaeus in "Berenice" until he became an increasingly skillful inquisitor into the dark recesses of the mind. Once he had discovered that he could lose his own individuality in a fictitious one, he had the basis on which to take advantage of what he had learned.

The year 1835 was crucial in the development of Poe's literary acumen; it was the year in which both "Berenice" and *Politian: An Unfinished Tragedy* were published. Mabbott as editor of the manuscript supplied the term "tragedy" in the title of *Politian*. When it appeared in 1835, Poe called it simply "Scenes from an Unpublished Drama." The fragments were not only never developed into a full-length play; they were never followed by the development of tragic characters, tragic views, and tragic forms characteristic of old world literature. "Berenice" was followed by "The Fall of the House of Usher," which continued Poe's interest in "terror — terror of the soul" as a thesis for fiction, and which dissociated his work from the death of tragedy as a genre. To develop, not a form for disguising autobiography as fiction but an alternate mode for the tragic as it was classically defined, meant that Poe had to pay more than lip service to the conscious force, the dominion of will over the unconscious forces and freedom of the imagination.

Politian was to have been the idealized account of a seduction, a marriage, and a murder that occurred in the state of Kentucky, but Poe made no effort to describe a local setting. The play begins with the direction: "ROME. A hall in a Palace." There is nothing, except perhaps the names chosen for the characters, that would suggest Rome. On the contrary, there is one descriptive passage in which the heroine, Lalage, proposes that she and Politian "fly" to the new world:

> Knowest thou the land
> With which all tongues are busy — a land new found —
> Miraculously found by one of Genoa —
> A thousand leagues within the golden west?
> A fairy land of flowers, and fruit, and sunshine,
> And crystal lakes, and over-arching forests,
> And mountains, around whose towering summits the winds
> Of Heaven untrammelled flow — which air to breathe
> Is Happiness now, and will be Freedom hereafter
> In days that are to come? [M 274, lines 65-74]

The passage, had Poe completed the drama, would probably have been ironic. At least, he would never again describe that barbarous region, in which he was born, as quite the earthly paradise it once had seemed from either a European or an innocent perspective. He was willing, nonetheless, to use the "new land" as a source of images and thematics before he was aware that he would not be a tragic poet.

Given the tastes of readers and the desire to transcend those tastes "in the air of democracy," he had the critical sense to become an American man of letters. A vast distance from the world of traditional heroes, and literature, he took the liberty to range as he wished according to principles that simultaneously limited him as he foraged, even scrounged for poetic ideas in a new world. Poe consequently made of it not just what he was but what it was also.

THE IMAGINATION OF A
GREAT LANDSCAPE

I appeal to you as a man that loves the same beauty which I adore—the beauty of the natural blue sky and the sunshiny earth. . . .

Poe to John Neal, 1829

I take SPACE to be the central fact to man born in America. . . . Something else than a stretch of earth—seas on both side, no barrier to contain as restless a thing as Western man was becoming in Columbus' day. Melville mounted. Poe dug in.

Charles Olson, *Call Me Ishmael*

1

To begin a description of a lost star with "O! nothing earthly . . ." as Poe begins the early poem *Al Aaraaf* (1829) and to hold literally to the point would be the end of the poem. In fact, it could, at most, have consisted of the words "O! nothing." Yet *Al Aaraaf* continues for over four hundred lines and is Poe's longest poem. In it he imagines a "world afar, afar —" both in time and space: life on a star "which appeared in the heavens [in 1572], . . . then as suddenly disappeared, and has never been seen since" (M 99). Poe describes "the wandering star" not only as a "world" but as "yon lovely Earth,/ Whence sprang the 'Idea of Beauty' into birth. . . ." Both the sidereal universe, an island between Heaven and Hell, and the abstract conception of beauty are realized in images of the phenomenal world. "The brilliance of earth," Wallace Stevens reminds us, "is the brilliance of every paradise" (*The Necessary Angel,* p. 77).

The earthly images of Poe's poetry tend, however, to be disregarded in critical attention to Poe's longing for supernal beauty, his desire to escape the dull realities of "eternal condor years," and his stress on the ideality of art. Even though there has been more than cursory interest in Poe's "lust for verisimilitude" and his "materialism,"[1] readers are tempted to take his dislike for "mere Flemish devotion to matter of fact," his cognizance of "subjective reality,"[2] and his "spiritualizing" of the material as the perspectives from which to approach his work. Finally, useful studies of literary influences and sources or echoes of the school of melancholy and the pervasive aesthetics of the sublime relevant to Poe do not necessitate consideration of the resemblance between the natural world and Poe's imagined worlds.

Yet, when Poe defined art as "the reproduction of what the Senses perceive in Nature through the veil of the soul" (H 16:164), he justified our approaching what he wrote from either the perspective of the nature that was perceived or the "veil of the soul" through which the sensory perceptions were filtered. Going on to say that the "mere imitation, however accurate, of what *is* in Nature, entitles no man to the sacred name of 'Artist,'" Poe insured the freedom to "reproduce" as the soul (psyche, mind) decided in relation to what the senses allowed. While he freed himself from mimesis, he recognized the dependence of the imagination on the given world. To approach Poe's work from an interest in that dependence is at once more simple-minded and treacherously complicated than "taking the veil of the soul" and disavowing the world seen through the veil. We cannot recover the reality of the world; all we have are the images seen through the veil, but Poe's landscape of a lost star provides a measure of his irrefragable use of the known to imagine the unknown.

Al Aaraaf, the birthplace of beauty, is in Wallace Stevens's phrase a "realm of resemblance." The opening lines of the poem establish the nature of that realm:

> O! nothing earthly save the ray
> (Thrown back from flowers) of Beauty's eye,
> As in those gardens where the day
> Springs from the gems of Circassy —
> O! nothing earthly save the thrill
> Of melody in woodland rill —
> . . . nothing of the dross of ours —
> Yet all the beauty — all the flowers . . . .
>
> [Part 1, lines 1-12]

The star, then, is an idealized place; the dross of our weary, unbright cinder, as Thomas Wolfe called earth, is washed away. The stellar landscape, conceived by an earth-bound mind, corresponds to splendors visible to that mind. On Al Aaraaf there are green fields, a "sheeny mountain," and a dim plain. There are groves of trees, a lone lake, clear springs, bright waterfalls, natural fountains, fair flowers in leaf and blossom. The flowers, from the gardens of the earth, are both cultivated and wild: sephalica, lilies, the lotus, bluebell, streamer (stream orchid), and tufted spray. The honied dew of the flowers is dropped from heaven; the flowers torture and madden the bee, perfume the night, and burst their hearts to sing their way to heaven.

Kneeling in a shrine of flowers, the goddess Nesace, maiden spirit of beauty, chants a vesper prayer to God, whose solemn voice pervades the air in response. (It will be almost a century before Wallace Stevens's

Madame Ste Ursule makes an offering of radishes and flowers to "the good Lord" who will hear her "low accord/ Half prayer and half ditty," and feel a subtle quiver that is "not heavenly love,/ Or pity."[3]) When Nesace's prayer is over, she rises

> . . . in the yellow night,
> The single-mooned eve! — on Earth we plight
> Our faith to one love — and one moon adore —
> The birth-place of young Beauty had no more.
> [Part 1, lines 151-54]

By day the air of the island star is golden and opaled; there are four bright suns, seas of light billowing densely, and rich clouds.

The palace of Nesace is high on a mountain of "rosy head that [,] towering far away/ Into the sunlit ether, caught the ray/ Of sunken suns at eve . . ." (part 2, lines 7-9). The architect for the building — the only one in the "landscape" — could have been Thomas Jefferson.[4] A pile of gorgeous columns is of Parian marble; a dome sits gently as a crown on the columns, and within the dome there is a window of one circular diamond.

> But on the pillars Seraph eyes have seen
> The dimness of this world: that greyish green
> That Nature loves the best for Beauty's grave
> Lurk'd in each cornice, round each architrave —
>
> And every sculptur'd cherub thereabout
> That from his marble dwelling peeréd out,
> Seem'd earthly in the shadow of his niche. . . .
> [Part 2, lines 28-34]

The sculptures, seeming earthly, have been transported from the old world.

Nesace, spirit that she is, runs with the "wild energy of wanton haste [,]/ Her cheeks . . . flushing, and her lips apart;/ And zone that clung around her gentle waist/ Had burst beneath the heaving of her heart" (part 2, lines 51-55). The slight disorder in her dress is a note that comes unexpectedly from Poe if we read the poem as a celebration of "nothing earthly." Writing to James Russell Lowell in 1844, Poe said, "I have no belief in spirituality. I think the word a *mere* word. No one has really a conception of spirit. We cannot imagine what is not" (O 1:257).

In *Al Aaraaf* Poe's conception of what *is* clearly begins with a distinction between natural phenomena and the "ghostlier demarcations" of ideal things:

> All Nature speaks, and ev'n ideal things
> Flap shadowy sounds from visionary wings —
> But ah! not so when . . . in realms on high
> The eternal voice of God is passing by;
> And the red winds are withering in the sky!
>
> [Part 1, lines 128-32]

Although the ideal is shadowy by comparison with the reality of God's nature, there is a correspondence between the ideal, that which is imagined, and the given world. Poe's use of the word "modell'd" in the song of Nesace to Ligeia is the crux of the relationship. The circumstances that evoke the song are familiar human ones. Nesace longs to rest; there is a silence upon material things, and a song springs from her spirit. The song is a tribute but also a charge to Ligeia, the soul and image of music. She is called to rise from her dreaming in the starlit hours and attend to her duty — the poet's duty — vigilance over "the strains" of "the music of things" or "the rhythmical number." Nesace sings:

> Ligeia! wherever
> Thy image may be,
> No image shall sever
> Thy music from thee.
> Thou hast bound many eyes
> In a dreamy sleep —
> But the strains still arise
> Which *thy* vigilance keep —
> The sound of the rain
> Which leaps down to the flower,
> And dances again
> In the rhythm of the shower —
> The murmur that springs
> From the growing of grass
> Are the music of things —
> But are modell'd, alas!
>
> [Part 2, lines 112-27]

Thereafter Ligeia is asked to awaken with her music the seraphs who have been lulled to rest by "the rhythmical number." The strains of that music are "modell'd." Poe does not mean that they are mundane copies of heavenly realities and the Platonic idea of beauty,[5] but are modeled in relation to the music of things (the sound and rhythm of the rain, and the murmur of the grass) in nature. The music is not necessarily mimetic;

Ligeia is, rather, required to listen to the harmonies of the natural world in composing her song. Such a directive is consistent with Poe's view that only God can create substantially; the "creative imagination" of the artist is the freedom of the mind to model or combine selectively from the perceptions of the given and its determinants. For Poe, the song, the poem, the fiction — the "modell'd" — is the ideal as opposed to reality. (This is the reason for the mournful "alas!") The principal terms in the aesthetic are the old Platonic ones — the words of the tribe — to which Poe has given "new" meaning.

The lines about the murmur that springs from the growing grass are among many examples of Poe's pleasure in freely using perceptions of known phenomena. Attributing the idea for the lines to an old English tale which he notes he is unable to obtain, Poe says he is quoting from memory: "The verie essence, and, as it were, springeheade, and origins of all musiche is the verie pleasaunte sounde which the trees of the forest do make when they growe" (M 110). Since the source has not yet been found, Poe may well have made it up, but the ultimate source of the point is an observable phenomenon in nature — trees do make sounds that can be heard if one listens to them when they are growing — and Poe has simply transferred that fact to the grass. In taking liberty with a "matter of fact," Poe makes it clear that Ligeia's song is not a naturalistic description of the sounds of nature, but an act of the mind rendering an imaginative "music of things."

All the visible universe, Baudelaire writes, is only a storehouse of images and signs to which the imagination will give a place and a relative value (or meaning). The world is a kind of pasture that the imagination should digest and transform.[6] Mixed as the metaphors are, they indicate Baudelaire's acknowledgment of the same sources that Poe depends upon when he talks about the work of art.

Baudelaire, as a poet, wanted particularly to seize the images and employ the signs of language to evoke or express hidden realities. When Poe, again in notes for *Al Aaraaf*, writes that he often "thought" he "could distinctly hear the sound of darkness as it stole over the horizon" (M 107), he distinguishes between the mind's response and the natural phenomenon which is subjectively transformed by the poet. Poe's aesthetic, then, provides for the power of the mind and simultaneously gives its subjective "reality" the status of the ideal. While the ideal is "shadowy," it has its own kind of force for the listener. Thus Poe writes:

> Sound loves to revel in a summer night:
> Witness the murmur of the grey twilight
> That stole upon the ear, in Eyraco,

Of many a wild star-gazer long ago —
That stealeth ever on the ear of him
Who, musing, gazeth on the distance dim,
And sees the darkness coming as a cloud —
Is not its form — its voice — most palpable and loud?

[Part 2, lines 40-47]

One thinks of Wallace Stevens's meditation on descending night and the human effort to arrange, deepen, and enchant that night in "The Idea of Order at Key West":

Words of the fragrant portals, dimly-starred,
And of ourselves and of our origins,
In ghostlier demarcations, keener sounds.

[*Collected Poems,* p. 130]

Poe, Baudelaire, and Stevens consciously evoke realms of resemblance. Poe, for all his imaginative flights, is still a poet of earth.

If Poe is a poet of earth when he imagines life — landscape and the spirits that people it — on a lost star, we can go on to ask in what ways he imagines the natural world that he knew most intimately, the American landscape.

2

William Cullen Bryant published in 1829 a sonnet to Thomas Cole, one of the landscape painters of the Hudson River school, upon Cole's departure to Europe. Cole's eyes, Bryant states, shall see the light of distant skies, yet the painter's heart shall bear to Europe

A living image of our own bright land . . .
Lone lakes — savannas where the bison roves —
    Rocks rich with summer garlands — solemn streams —
    Skies, where the desert eagle wheels and screams —
Spring bloom and autumn blaze of boundless groves.

Bryant anticipates that "fair scenes shall greet" Cole wherever he goes in Europe — "fair,/ But different." Bryant is explicit about the difference: "everywhere the trace of men,/ Paths, homes, graves, ruins, from the lowest glen/ To where life shrinks from the fierce Alpine air. . . ." The poet advises the painter to gaze on the European scene "till the tears shall dim thy sight,/ But keep that earlier, wilder image bright."[7]

Poe, reviewing the poetry of Bryant for the *Southern Literary Messenger* of January 1837, cited the lines "Paths, homes, graves, ruins, from the lowest glen/ To where life shrinks from the fierce Alpine air" as worthy of praise, but thought the concluding ones feeble (H 9:295). Poe gave no reasons for the opinion. Perhaps he disliked the meter or the didactic and admonishing tone of the final lines; perhaps he shared the image of a congenial European landscape for which even the exuberant, if not chauvinistic, Bryant longed, but was less appreciative of the sentimental tears or "the living image of our bright land." Poe could hardly have failed, however, to be aware that Bryant had articulated briefly, clearly, and typically a conception of a difference between the European and American landscape — the one in which there was "everywhere the trace of men" and the other, whatever its charms, prescribing the adjectives "lone," "solemn," "boundless," and "wilder." The American conception of the emptiness and vastness of space does not hiss at us in the Bryant poem, but the screams of the eagle pierce it, and Poe possesses it. Planning near the end of his life a book on "The Living Writers of America," Poe made some notes on that conception. "Distant subjects," he said, are "in fact the most desirable. . . . The true poet is less affected by the absolute contemplation than [by] the imagination of a great landscape" (M 189).

The ambiguities of the phrases "distant subjects" and "the imagination of a great landscape" do not justify the frequent assumption that Poe's landscapes are "out of space." Furthermore, the distinction between "the absolute contemplation" and "the imagination of a great landscape" depends upon the constant "a great landscape." As Wallace Stevens has said, "The world of the poet depends on the world he has contemplated."[8] A world that Poe of necessity contemplated, except for five years of childhood in England, was that great landscape, America. The engaging question is what did he make of it?

The question can be explored by a comparison of Poe's treatment of landscape with characteristics of the subject in several analogous works. Both Poe and Thomas Moore, for instance, wrote poems evoked by the same place in Virginia; Poe, Byron, and Thomas Cole depict the ruins of the Coliseum of Rome, which Poe had not visited; Poe and Baudelaire treat landscape in dream poems that are similar in structure, mode, and numerous details; Poe and Rousseau recount reveries stimulated by walks in nature: all within a period of literary history that may be said to have begun with Rousseau and to be typified by a pleasure in contemplating landscape. The range of examples includes a number of variables, among them Poe's own changes and experiments in the use of setting throughout his life as a writer. The examples are fortuitous, however, because they include: (a) an Irish tourist's and a native American's response to an American scene; (b) English and American responses to European ruins; (c) surreal landscapes by an American and a French poet; and (d) a European and an American contemplating solitary landscapes which are, respectively, Swiss and American. The differences in perceptions clarify some of the elusive qualities in Poe's vision.

3

In Poe's first published work, *Tamerlane and Other Poems* (1827), "The Lake" is inspired by a native scene, Drummond Pond, near Norfolk, Virginia. The poem is also indebted to "A Ballad: The Lake of the Dismal Swamp," written by twenty-four-year-old Thomas Moore when he was spending a summer (1803) in Norfolk.[9] But Poe's poem evokes a much emptier and lonelier place than the lonely scene in the Irish poet's ballad.

Moore's ballad was suggested, according to his note, by a story of a young man who, having lost his mind upon the death of a girl he loved, disappeared. Since he frequently said that the girl was not dead but had gone to the Dismal Swamp, it was supposed he followed her and died there. Moore's poem begins in the voice of the bereaved young man consoling himself:

> "They made her a grave, too cold and damp
>   "For a soul so warm and true;
> "And she's gone to the Lake of the Dismal Swamp,
> "Where, all night long, by a fire-fly lamp,
>   "She paddles her white canoe.
>
> "And her fire-fly lamp I soon shall see,
>   "And her paddle I soon shall hear;
> "Long and loving our life shall be,
> "And I'll hide the maid in a cypress tree,
>   "When the footstep of death is near."

The action of the poem and the isolated scene follow:

> Away to the Dismal Swamp he speeds —
>   His path was rugged and sore,
> Through tangled juniper, beds of reeds,
> Through many a fen, where the serpent feeds,

And man never trod before.

And, when on the earth he sunk to sleep,
     If slumber his eyelids knew,
He lay, where the deadly vine doth weep
Its venomous tear and nightly steep
     The flesh with blistering dew!

And near him the she-wolf stirred the brake,
     And the copper-snake breathed in his ear,
Till he starting cried, from his dream awake,
"Oh! when shall I see the dusky Lake,
     "And the white canoe of my dear?"

He saw the Lake, and a meteor bright
     Quick over its surface played —
"Welcome," he said, "my dear-one's light!"
And the dim shore echoed, for many a night,
     The name of the death-cold maid.

Till he hollowed a boat of the birchen bark,
     Which carried him off from shore;
Far, far he followed the meteor spark,
The wind was high and the clouds were dark,
     And the boat returned no more.

The dramatic action of the poem is over. Moore, however, adds a comforting last verse:

     But oft, from the Indian hunter's camp
          This lover and maid so true
     Are seen at the hour of midnight damp
          To cross the Lake by a fire-fly lamp,
     And paddle their white canoe!

Back of Moore's accomplished poem is an Irish folk imagination; yet that imagination has become too literary. The poet hardly does more than play with loss and loneliness and terror. The ballad is "eerie" without being eerie; it is, rather, genial and pleasant; in its illusion of enchantment it verges on the fanciful. Although many of its details are pretty, at least one of them — "the deadly vine" that weeps its "venomous tear" — anticipates Poe, and Moore indeed outdoes him in the painful description of the vine's steeping flesh "with blistering dew." The Irish poet-tourist seems to have transformed a tangle of honeysuckle and woodbine (with which the swamp still abounds) into poison ivy as if to compensate for the fact that the ballad's swamp is almost as tame as it is wild. Nonetheless, the poison ivy is forgotten in the image of a companionable human presence that unites the lovers; but even recent descriptions of the great swamp, diminishing as it is, do not give the feeling that human encounters are frequent there.[10]

Poe's poem, "The Lake," is verbally less accomplished than Moore's ballad, but is also the poem of a young man (not over eighteen years old) attracted by a similar theme in relation to the same setting. In contrast to the graceful whimsy of Moore, the American poet begins awkwardly, recalls the place, gropes to express the nuances of feeling it evoked, and ends in an elegiac strain:

> In youth's spring, it was my lot
> To haunt of the wide earth a spot
> The which I could not love the less;
> So lovely was the loneliness
> Of a wild lake, with black rock bound,
> And the tall trees that tower'd around.
> But when the night had thrown her pall
> Upon that spot — as upon all,
> And the wind would pass me by
> In its stilly melody,
> My infant spirit would awake
> To the terror of the lone lake.
> Yet that terror was not fright —
> But a tremulous delight,
> And a feeling undefin'd,
> Springing from a darken'd mind.
> Death was in that poison'd wave
> And in its gulf a fitting grave
> For him who thence could solace bring
> To his dark imagining;
> Whose wild'ring thought could even make
> An Eden of that dim lake. [M 84-85]

A sense of space beyond that in which the scene of the poem is located and the implication of frequent visits to the scene as well as the unequivocal statement of pleasure in the loneliness and wildness of the lake distinguish the opening of Poe's poem from Moore's initial focus on a man speaking. Poe's scene is so quiet one can hear the wind blowing. With a few bold strokes Poe suggests something overpowering about the place encountered by an infant spirit awakening to the terror of the lone lake. Moore's pleasing visual sense of fireflies, beds of reeds, copper-snake, white canoe, birch bark, bright meteor, although the clouds are dark — all the careful little details are lost in the darkness that comes over Poe's landscape.

A darkened mind trembles in the darkness. How can the trembling be expressed? It is terror, clearly distinguished from fright but modulated with a tenuously fearful delight and attenuated by a feeling that cannot be defined. If there is any light in the poem it is the darkened mind's awareness of the subtleties of imaginative longing in that solitary place. Sensing full well the terror and the reality of death there, the lonely person evokes, not an illusion of a companionable human presence, but the memory of another darkened mind, whose name is lost — the only identification is the "him" who died there — and whose heroism was that his "wild'ring thought could even make/ An Eden of that dim lake."

Poe's subjects are isolated in space and time. They are distanced by memory, the persona's reminiscence of having "haunted" the wild scene and of being haunted by his silent contemplation of both the landscape and its effect on another bewildered imagination. The poem's power is in the imaginative integration of these melancholy subjects which are terminated in the implied question as well as in praise of an Edenic view of the troubled waters of the new world. The poem consciously reveals the independent imagination brooding upon a great landscape.

One is not surprised to find that Poe, speaking of kinds of paintings appropriate for interior decoration in "The Philosophy of Furniture" (1840), recommended "landscapes of an imaginative cast — such as . . . the lake of the Dismal Swamp of [John G.] Chapman." It was an image of Poe's "lone lake," a wild landscape, to which he responded in an allusive lyric at least ten years before he cited Bryant's charge to Cole.

4

An example of American interest in the geographically distant subject is Poe's poem "The Coliseum" (1833). Since Poe never visited Rome, the poem depended on a number of sources. A primary one, generally overlooked and difficult to substantiate, must have been Poe's home-grown imagination. Poe himself, in a note for *Tamerlane* (1827), teasingly suggests to the literal-minded a way in which a writer about distant subjects works: "I must beg the reader's pardon for making Tamerlane, a Tartar of the fourteenth century, speak in the same language as a Boston gentleman of the nineteenth: but of the Tartar mythology we have little information" (M 31). Or again, with respect to the use of an image of the dayflower, he notes that he has never known its botanic name, but "It blooms beautifully in the day-light, . . . withers towards evening, and by night its leaves appear totally shrivelled and dead. I have forgotten, however, to mention in the text, that it lives again in the morning. If it will not flourish in Tartary, I must be forgiven for carrying it thither" (M 39). Tongue in cheek or not, Poe must have carried a slight American accent, an American imagination, to a subject which also appealed to Thomas Cole, the American painter. Cole's "Interior of the Colosseum, Rome" (probably painted in 1832) and his notes following a visit to the scene (in 1832) help to characterize the native influences in Poe's imagination. When their depictions of the historical ruins are compared with a description of the Coliseum in Byron's *Manfred* (1817), a source for Poe's poem,[11] the Americans have much in common.

In the dramatic poem *Manfred* Byron begins the final episode with Manfred alone in the tower of his Alpine castle. It is a beautiful night; the stars are out and the moon is above the "snow-shining mountains." Manfred, soliloquizing, recalls such a night in his youth when he stood within the Coliseum's walls:

> . . .'Midst the chief relics of almighty Rome;
> The trees which grew along the broken arches
> Waved dark in the blue midnight, and the stars
> Shone through the rents of ruin; from afar
> The watch-dog bayed beyond the Tiber; and
> More near from out the Caesars' palace came
> The owl's long cry, and, interruptedly,
> Of distant sentinels the fitful song
> Begun and died upon the gentle wind.
> Some cypresses beyond the time-worn breach
> Appeared to skirt the horizon, yet they stood
> Within a bowshot.

Rome is almighty, but the relic of the Coliseum does not loom large, or excite a feeling of unusual grandeur. In spite of the Gothic owl, the ruin is placed rather casually within the city — "from afar/ The watch-dog bayed beyond the Tiber"; and sentinels could be heard singing now and again. Although the cypress trees look a long way off, they are actually, Manfred knows, very close. There is nothing particularly awesome about the place. The trees growing along the arches are dark, but it is a good clear midnight. The human history and the life of nature are merged almost as if they were one in the description:

> Where the Caesars dwelt
> And dwell the tuneless birds of night, amidst
> A grove which springs through levelled battlements,
> And twines its roots with the imperial hearths,
> Ivy usurps the laurel's place of growth;
> But the gladiators' bloody Circus stands,
> A noble wreck in ruinous perfection,
> While Caesar's chambers, and the Augustan halls,
> Grovel on earth in indistinct decay.

Nature is not ignored, or humanized, but it is joined with the domestic scene which is "in indistinct decay." The ruins are noble; they project a human tragedy. Manfred's regret is for the end of human life once lived in the place when it was not in ruins, and for him it is as if the gladiators' Circus were still blood-stained from a recent sports event. The lines that follow are an imaginative "restoration" of the human spirit in an atmosphere of regenerative light:

> And thou didst shine, thou rolling Moon, upon
> All this, and cast a wide and tender light,
> Which softened down the hoar austerity
> Of rugged desolation, and filled up,
> As 'twere anew, the gaps of centuries;
> Leaving that beautiful which still was so,
> And making that which was not — till the place
> Became religion, and the heart ran o'er
> With silent worship of the Great of old —
> The dead, but sceptred, Sovereigns, who still rule
> Our spirits from their urns.

The aura of moonlight softens the stark desolation and renders it aesthetically pleasing. In contrast to the lack of awe in Manfred's actual description of the ruins, his veneration is for the great sovereigns he has taken as exemplars, sceptred and brought back to life to worship for their strength. Though dead, they "still rule/ Our spirits." Hence, the place became "religion" for him. Manfred himself is soon to refuse to give his soul to opposing "spirits" that come to demand it for his crimes. He sends them back to their Hell, takes upon himself the responsibility for having been his own destroyer, and dies as if he were an existential hero. Manfred is a fine match for the ruins of the Coliseum. It is, appropriately, to him a place of burial — the urns — for the ashes of powerful men.

Poe's poem is a dramatic monologue. The hero is, like Manfred, inspired

by his visit to the Coliseum, but he is no existential equal for the ruins.
He *is* the religious pilgrim and begins by an invocation:

> Type of the antique Rome! Rich reliquary
> Of lofty contemplation left to Time
> By buried centuries of pomp and power!
> At length — at length — after so many days
> Of weary pilgrimage and burning thirst,
> (Thirst for the springs of lore that in thee lie,)
> I kneel, an altered and an humble man,
> Amid thy shadows, and so drink within
> My very soul thy grandeur, gloom, and glory!
>
> [M 228-29]

The pilgrim immediately suggests the monumental scale of the structure
when he speaks of it as an object of "lofty contemplation left to Time";
stressing the long journey to reach the reliquary, he also places it in an
expanse far greater than the city landscape of Byron's description.
Furthermore, the pilgrim does not stand up to the monument, but kneels
humbly in awe amid the shadows. It is not an exaggeration to say that he
is dwarfed by the grandeur, gloom, and glory he has come to share. He
continues in an exclamatory tone:

> Vastness! and Age! and Memories of Eld!
> Silence! and Desolation! and dim Night!
> I feel ye now — I feel ye in your strength —
> O spells more than e'er Judaean King
> Taught in the garden of Gethsemane!
> O charms more potent than the rapt Chaldee
> Ever drew down from the quiet stars!

The emotions are strong. The vastness, the silence, the dim night open
the awareness not to the commonplace watchdog and guards close enough
that they can be heard, but to associations with mysteries and powers of
persons, places, and civilizations distant or different from the Rome of
the Caesars — the king of the Jews (in Gethsemane), nameless Semitic
priests, and astrologers of Babylonia. These associations serve as points
of contrast with the feeling of power the pilgrim seeks in the sacred place;
and the feeling is experienced, but it is momentary, as it was not for
Manfred. Nor is the desolation softened, as it was in Byron's poem, by
a lambent light that sustains the beauty of the ruins. Heroes, their ladies,
their monarch, the insignia and conspicuous displays of human power and

privilege — all are remembered, if not fondly at least vividly, in a scene not unlike Hollywood spectaculars:

> Here, where a hero fell, a column falls!
> Here, where the mimic eagle glared in gold,
> A midnight vigil holds the swarthy bat!
> Here, where the dames of Rome their gilded hair
> Waved to the wind, now wave the reed and thistle!
> Here, where on golden throne the monarch lolled,
> Glides, spectre-like, unto his marble home,
> Lit by the wan light of the horned moon,
> The swift and silent lizard of the stones!

The action quickens: where a hero fell, a column falls. The chiaroscuro is bold. A "swarthy bat" (even more Gothic than Byron's owl), the graceful reed, the straggling thistle, and a "spectre-like" lizard that glides among the stones are counterfoils to bright images of historic life that has now disappeared from the place — a symbolic eagle of gold, women with gilded hair, and an indolent monarch on a golden throne. The memory of garish human life is usurped repeatedly by a quickened nature. The images of that nature are not as commonplace as they are eerie. Poe's personal taste for the gaudy and his flair for the macabre may account for the imagined details. There is, however, an American light that does not soften the scene even when the poet says it is lit by a wan crescent moon. There is also a sharp break in historical continuity, a history with which Byron's Manfred is at home. Unlike Manfred's more restrained description in which ruins, nature, and human elements blend perceptibly as well as imperceptibly together, Poe's scene is one of clear contrasts between remembered human history and primeval nature or prehistory to which the ruins have returned.

The visual details of the next stanza, however, almost suggest in their reliance on architectural terminology that Poe's pilgrim has a tourist's guidebook to Rome in hand:

> But stay! these walls — these ivy-clad arcades —
> These mouldering plinths — these sad and blackened shafts —
> These vague entablatures — this crumbling frieze —
> These shattered cornices — this wreck — this ruin —
> These stones — alas! these gray stones — are they all —
> All of the famed, and the colossal left
> By the corrosive Hours to Fate and me?

The description decidedly suggests an illustration or a black and white reproduction of a painting of the ruins. But Poe's is not primarily a beautiful or comforting scene; his poem expresses, rather, a melancholy sense of loss, of the abandoned, of empty and pervasive desolation.

The brooding pilgrim of necessity asks whether this is all there is for him among these ruins with their rich associations. He receives a poignant reply from an obstructing surface:

> "Not all" — the Echoes answer me — "not all!
> "Prophetic sounds and loud, arise forever
> "From us, and from all Ruin, unto the wise,
> "As melody from Memnon to the Sun.
> "We rule the hearts of mightiest men — we rule
> "With a despotic sway all giant minds.
> "We are not impotent — we pallid stones.
> "Not all our power is gone — not all our fame —
> "Not all the magic of our high renown —
> "Not all the wonder that encircles us —
> "Not all the mysteries that in us lie —
> "Not all the memories that hang upon
> "And cling around about us as a garment,
> "Clothing us in a robe of more than glory."

The Echoes, however fatally attractive the despotic powers and glorious memories they express, are more ambiguous than the clear voice of Manfred. Manfred's commanding presence, so vigorously matched to the ruins of the Coliseum, influenced Poe's questioning and listening (weary and humble) pilgrim. But the echoes he hears explode and die in the ear. Their irregular rhythms and broken melodies insist, repeatedly insist, "Not all . . . not all. . . ." No matter how pallid the stones, they are not impotent: theirs is an aura of mystery and the voice of secrets which are not man's to command. Poe's is a pilgrim moved by fancies that are curled around the images and cling to ancient greatness and memories of inexpressible glory. The final sentences of the poem belong to the prophetic echoes, not the pilgrim who mediates an American nostalgia for the magnificence of distant, ancient ruins and the traditions that he cannot recover since at their most prophetic — or insistent — they are for him only echoes.

Thomas Cole, tourist, writing March 4, 1832, from Rome, says, "The things that most affect me, in Rome, are the antiquities."[12] Later, on May 14 at Naples, he writes in his journal: "I left Rome almost without making a memorandum of the many objects of interest I there saw. . . .

I must devote an hour to the 'City of the soul' . . . . From the great multitude of wondrous things, I would select the Colosseum as the object that affected me the most" (pp. 115-16).

Cole's recollection is closer in tone and perspective to Poe[13] than to Byron's way of viewing the ruin. "It is," Cole remarks, "stupendous, yet beautiful in its destruction. From the broad arena within, it rises around you, arch above arch, broken and desolate. . . ." Finding it beautiful, as did Manfred, Cole nevertheless sees it as immense and lofty — just as Poe had imagined it. And while the painter does not kneel like Poe's pilgrim, there is no sense of Byronic stature equal to the ruins; they are not a place in which Cole takes on heroic proportions. With Byron's advantage of having been there, Cole notes: the structure is "mantled in many parts with the laurustinus, the acanthus, and numerous other plants and flowers, exquisite both for their colour and fragrance." Poe's "reed and thistle" are not there, but the American painter's sense of the ruined monument is striking in its resemblance to Poe's: "It looks more like a work of nature than of man; for the regularity of art is lost, in a great measure, in dilapidation, and the luxuriant herbage, clinging to its ruins as if 'to mouth its distress,' completes the illusion." Poe's echoing stones do not mourn as unequivocally as does Cole's mouthing vegetation, but both writers betray a reliance on inhuman sources to express emotions in contrast to Manfred's cognizance of human power and the spirits of sovereign men in the solitude. For the Americans, the scene is obviously much lonelier and much emptier. Cole heard neither barking dog nor sentinel's songs.

The landscape painter's description continues as if he is looking at mountain scenery: "Crag rises over crag, green and breezy summits mount into the sky." Then he remembers history: "To walk beneath its crumbling walls, to climb its shattered steps, to wander through its long, arched passages, to tread in the footsteps of Rome's ancient kings, to muse upon its broken height, is to lapse into sad, though not unpleasing meditation." Cole's "crumbling walls" and "shattered steps" or Poe's "crumbling frieze" and "shattered cornices" involve adjectives anyone might use among the ruins. More important than similarities in detail, however, are Poe and Cole's disinclination to domesticate the scene. Cole thinks of the footsteps of Rome's kings, but he does not, like Byron's Manfred, fill up the gap of centuries and bring history back alive. Like Poe's pilgrim, Cole enjoys the melancholy contemplation of the ruins; Cole has, moreover, an ambivalent attitude toward their significance.

After recalling the Roman scene in the light of day, Cole records a further experience in which the vigor of his imagination is evident. The painter's response is one that Poe would have appreciated. Cole wrote:

But he who would see and feel the grandeur of the Colosseum must spend his hour there, at night, when the moon is shedding over it its magic splendour. Let him ascend to its higher terraces, at that pensive time, and gaze down into the abyss, or hang his eye upon the ruinous ridge, where it gleams in the moonrays, and charges boldly against the deep blue heaven. The mighty spectacle, mysterious and dark, opens beneath the eye more like some awful dream than an earthly reality, — a vision of the valley and shadow of death, rather than the substantial work of man. Could man, indeed, have ministered either to its erection or its ruin?

The ambience is that of Manfred's moonlight and blue midnight, but the light is strong and the awe is like Poe's. Cole's is a darkened mind:

As I mused upon its great circumference, I seemed to be sounding the depths of some volcanic crater whose fires, long extinguished, had left the ribbed and blasted rocks to the wild-flower and the ivy. In a sense, the fancy is a truth: it was once the crater of human passions; there their terrible fires blazed forth with desolating power, and the thunder of the eruption shook the skies. But now all is still desolation.

Poe's sentient stones have undergone a volcanic change. Less nostalgic than Poe's Echoes, Cole's rhetoric of violence directed against "human passions" derives entirely from nature.

Poe's images of violence also often derive from nature. If there are only spectral traces of such imagery in "The Coliseum," Poe is an acknowledged master of metaphors of the abyss, the valley and shadow of death, volcanic crater, terrible fires blazing forth with desolating power, and thunder that shook the skies. And Poe might have written Cole's sentence: "But now all is still desolation."

Cole, also like Poe, listens for nuances that would attenuate the vision of a "mighty spectacle": mysterious, dark, awful. Having heard them, the painter ends his notes by remembering: "In the morning the warbling of birds makes the quiet air melodious; in the hushed and holy twilight, the low chanting of monkish solemnities soothes the startled ear." Byron would hardly have been surprised by the monks' presence; Poe does not imagine it.

Cole's turbulent night vision, which he attempts to palliate by referring to it not only as a vision but a fancy, is not the subject of his painting "Interior of the Colosseum."[14] The painting is in the keen, hard light of day. There are the broken columns, shadows, sad and blackened shafts, although the gray and more pallid stones of Poe's poem are burnished. There is the "crumbling" and "shattered" quality of the ruins sometimes softened by natural vegetation which Byron, Poe, and Cole mention in differing ways. The structure of the ruin dominates the width of the canvas (eighteen and three-fourths feet) and looks almost like a long range of ragged mountains, the highest of which is barren and rough. The "mountains" closest to the eye rise straight up darkly from the ground, but the highest one, more distant, recedes slightly and grayly toward the left top of the canvas where it occupies a large portion of the wide, clear sky above the broken ledges of rock. One feels that some of the rock is apt to crumble and fall from one of the jutting crags. In spite of the fact that Cole has almost returned the ruins to nature, he holds to historical fact and places in the center light of the interior ground a dark crucifix which rises a little higher than any of the standing columns. Two white-robed monks stand just to either side of the base of the cross. They are so small that they are almost specter-like. (The monks are, in fact, only one-thirteenth of the height of the canvas, which is ten and one-eighth feet.) They are matched by two or three equally small figures apparently approaching an arch just behind the crucifix. All the human figures are less striking than a great white bird with a darkened crown stationed on a broken architrave at a height matching that of the peak of the cross.

If Cole's are not quite Poe's broken melodies, Cole's memories in both the notes and painting of the Coliseum are tantalizingly close to them. The differences between them argue only for their individuality, just as some of the differences between Poe and Byron argue for theirs. Poe and Cole, nonetheless, share the attention given to a wild, uncultivated, or unrestrained nature; an awesome appreciation of colossal size; the perception of intense, hard light; an awareness of a break in historical continuity; a sense of solitude as opposed to the casual human presence that can be taken for granted; and the diminution of man within the scene whose natural elements are sentient. These similarities between them and their failure to follow Byron's exaltation of the human sovereignty that pervades Manfred's reminiscence of the ruins reflect an American imagination — even when Poe knew Byron's poem and probably did not know Cole's painting. When Bryant writes of Europe that there is "everywhere the trace of men," he merely glimpses the difference between the primal new and the primal old world that Cole and Poe bring together.

5

"Now, do you understand why," Charles Baudelaire writes "in the midst of the frightful solitude which surrounds me, I have understood Edgar Poe's genius so well. . . ?"[15] The French poet's singular devotion to the work of the American writer is well known. Poe's literary influence on Baudelaire is less certain. ("I," Baudelaire remarks, "am being accused, I, of imitating Edgar Poe: Do you know why I translated Poe so patiently? Because he was like me."[16]) There are, however, transpositions of images, conceptions, and occasional phrasing from Poe to Baudelaire. In one draft of a preface for the 1861 edition of *Les Fleurs du mal*, Baudelaire himself includes: "Notes on my plagiarisms: . . . Edgar Poe (2 passages)."[17] And at least one poem, "Parisian Dream" (first published in 1860), is obviously indebted to Poe's "Dream-Land" (1844).

Since Poe's dream landscape has been significant in the attitude of readers toward the subject of setting in his work and since Baudelaire not only felt himself surrounded by solitude but also identified with Poe, it is illuminating to consider "Dream-Land" (M 343–45) in relation to the dream poem by Baudelaire.

Poe's poem begins with a short narrative passage:

> By a route obscure and lonely,
> Haunted by ill angels only,
> Where an Eidolon, named Night,
> On a black throne reigns upright,
> I have reached these lands but newly
> From an ultimate dim Thule —
> From a wild weird clime that lieth, sublime,
> Out of Space — out of Time.

The "I" of the poem is the lone traveler recently arrived in "these lands." Having differentiated grammatically between "these lands" and "Dream-Land," Poe makes clear in the refrain that "these lands" are "home": "I have wandered home but newly/ From this ultimate dim Thule." (The line will be answered a decade later in Whitman's dream work "The Sleepers" [1855], which begins,"I wander all night in my vision.") Poe's refrain, distinguishing between "home lands" and Thule, uses the common figure of the journey for the transition from an awakened state to sleep as well as from sleep to wakefulness. The route is obscure, lonely, and haunted; the country of sleep and dreams is a vast one ruled by a phantom king, Night. The chief interest of the poem is the traveler's memory of the sights in the country; the weak phrase "but newly" (which should have been excised as a rhyme) affirms the immediacy of the experience in mind, and the immediacy is given force in the account of what the traveler recalls.

The land, designated by the Greek name for an undetermined region (Iceland, Shetland, Norway, or Scandinavia?) and described as "a wild weird" tract, lies "sublime/ Out of Space – out of Time." The uncertainty about the region to which Thule was applied makes Poe's choice of it appropriate for the dream country, but the wild, dynamic imagery in the dreamer's description of the landscape comes from nineteenth-century American nature.[18] The qualities of obscurity, power, privation, vastness, duration, difficulty of access, and perhaps even magnificence that characterize the sublime landscape are also relevant to the traveler's account of the dream experience. Poe does not customarily use the term "sublime" in describing a scene; in fact, there is no other instance of it in his poetry of landscape. Poe does write, in *Eureka,* that

> he who from the top of Aetna casts his eyes leisurely around is affected chiefly by the *extent* and *diversity* of the scene. Only by a rapid whirling on his heel could he hope to comprehend the panorama in the sublimity of its *oneness*. But as . . . *no* man has thought of whirling on his heel, so no man has ever taken into his brain the full uniqueness of the prospect. . . . [H 16:186]

The narrator of "The House of Usher," speaking of the unrelieved gloom of his response to the house, says his dreariness of thought could not be tortured into "aught of the sublime" (H 3:273). The sense Poe seems to observe in the uses of the word is the value of it as a phenomenon setting in motion states of the mind – or what Edmund Burke spoke of as turning "the soul in upon itself." In relying on the term in "Dream-Land," Poe's perspective is subliminal, that is, between the eighteenth-century aesthetics of the sublime and the twentieth-century mode of the surrealists.

Just as the surrealist must state a reality he then partially destroys or violates, Poe depends primarily on landscape familiar to him for the phantasmagoria the traveler describes:

> Bottomless vales and boundless floods,
> And chasms, and caves, and Titan woods,
> With forms that no man can discover
> For the dews that drip all over;
> Mountains toppling evermore
> Into seas without a shore;
> Seas that restlessly aspire,

> Surging, unto skies of fire;
> Lakes that endlessly outspread
> Their lone waters — still and chilly
> With the snows of the lolling lily.
> By the lakes that thus outspread
> Their lone water, lone and dead, —
> Their sad waters, sad and chilly
> With the snows of the lolling lily, —
> By the mountains — near the river
> Murmuring lowly, murmuring ever, —
> By the grey woods, — by the swamp
> Where the toad and the newt encamp, —
> By the dismal tarns and pools
>   Where dwell the Ghouls, —
> By each spot the most unholy . . . .

While the rhythms pall (sometimes the chant is genuine and sometimes it is a banal lilt), the scene itself is daringly conceived. It glimpses great distances, great forests, heavy dews, an unlimited supply of mountains, a dismal swamp, "water never formed to mind or voice," "high horizons, mountainous atmospheres of sky and sea." A "land . . . still unstoried, artless, unenhanced," it is primeval, unconsecrated, uncultivated, and uninhabited except by toads, newts, and ghouls. These are Poe's "living images" of a dream land bright with the "skies of fires" and "the snows of the lolling lily," but they have their origin in his native land hardly as distant as a dim Thule.

It may be objected that the landscape is not the major subject of the poem; the surreal images of the setting, however, are more charged with energy than the passage which follows the description of the land:

> There the traveller meets aghast
> Sheeted Memories of the Past —
> Shrouded forms that start and sigh
> As they pass the wanderer by —
> White-robed forms of friends long given,
> In agony, to the Earth — and Heaven.

These ghostly forms are the only vestiges of human life in the landscape, and they pass the traveler by. The poem then lapses into consideration of responses to the dream experience:

> For the heart whose woes are legion
> 'T is a peaceful, soothing region —
> For the spirit that walks in shadow
> O! it is an Eldorado!
> But the traveller, travelling through it,
> May not — dare not openly view it;
> Never its mysteries are exposed
> To the weak human eye unclosed;
> So wills its King, who hath forbid
> The uplifting of the fringed lid;
> And thus the sad Soul that here passes
> Beholds it but through darkened glasses.

The discursive passages on the psychological and physical effects of dreams seem a failure of imagination, as does the poet's return to the point already established in the opening verse: the King of Night rules the land, and the awakened subject's memory of it. The soul may be sad because of the frustrating limits placed on the human perception and understanding in contrast to the intense clarity of the dream landscape. The final lines of the poem bear the burden of the restive mind traveling by the route "obscure and lonely," which counterpoints the subliminal power of the dream imagery. The poem's conclusion, the traveler's announcement that he has arrived "home," is prosaically safe and downright dull:

> By a route obscure and lonely,
> Haunted by ill angels only,
> Where an Eidolon, named NIGHT
> On a black throne reigns upright,
> I have wandered home but newly
> From this ultimate dim Thule.

In "Rêve parisien" Baudelaire adapts the structure of Poe's poem, copies words from it, and transforms physical phenomena in the manner of "Dream-Land." This is the range of what Baudelaire calls "the plagiarisms." He begins by explaining subject and scene:

> De ce terrible paysage,
> Tel que jamais mortel n'en vit,
> Ce matin encore l'image,
> Vague et lointaine, me ravit.

> The vague and faraway (distant in time
> and space, dreamy) image of that ter-
> rible landscape, such as mortal man has
> never seen, this morning still enraptures me.

Le sommeil est plein de miracles!
Par un caprice singulier,
J'avais banni de ces spectacles
Le végétal irrégulier,

> Sleep is full of miracles!
> By a strange caprice,
> I had banished from this scene
> the irregular vegetation,

Et, peintre fier de mon génie,
Je savourais dans mon tableau
L'enivrante monotonie
Du métal, du marbre et de l'eau.

> And fine painter with my genius (genie),
> I savored in my picture
> the intoxicating monotony
> of metal, of marble and of water.

Although Baudelaire distances the dream landscape, he is more quickly in it and suggests that he has flicked it on in his mind, not that he has wandered through great distances to reach it. The dreamer's mastery over the images further suggests that even in depicting the dream process as vagarious Baudelaire unconsciously has a different perception of landscape; Poe's traveler has no easy dominance over great spaces and in this sense is much more the little man in the big picture. Baudelaire's title does not mean that the dream landscape is Parisian, but that the dreamer escapes from the city. Yet the dreamer's banishment of vegetation and intoxication with images of metal, marble, and water anticipate the surreal city-in-the-sea and sea-in-the-city images which are in contrast with the American poet's surreal natural landscape. Baudelaire's dream world is nonetheless powerful:

Babel d'escaliers et d'arcades,
C'était un palais infini,
Plein de bassins et de cascades
Tombant dans l'or mat ou bruni;

Babel of stairs and arcades,
it was an infinite palace
full of pools and cascades
falling in dull or burnished gold;

Et des cataractes pesantes,
Comme des rideaux de cristal,
Se suspendaient, éblonissantes
A des murailles de métal.

And heavy cataracts,
like curtains of crystal,
hung dazzling
on walls of metal.

Non d'arbres, mais de colonades
Les étangs dormants s'entouraient,
Où de gigantesques naïades,
Comme des femmes, se miraient.

The motionless (still) lakes were
surrounded, not by trees, but
by colonnades, where gigantic naiads,
like women, mirrored themselves.

Des nappes d'eau s'épanchaient, bleues,
Entre des quais roses et verts,
Pendant des millions de lieues,
Vers les confins de l'univers;

Sheets of water spread out, blue,
between the red and green quays,
along millions of leagues toward
the limits (the ends) of the universe;

C'étaient des pierres inouïes
Et des flots magiques; c'étaient
D'immenses glaces éblouies
Par tout ce qu'elles reflétaient!

There were strange (unheard of)
stones and magic waves; there were
immense mirrors dazzled
by all they reflected!

Seascape as well as landscape, reaching beyond the confines of palace and

harbors, indicating infinite spaces, the dream also derives from the architectural grandeurs of ancient civilization. Stairs, arcades, palaces, colonnades, whatever the confusion of structures, replace Poe's valleys, caves,
woods, mountains; naiads are alive and exotically although narcissistically
well, not Halloween ghosts of memory.

As solitary as Poe's traveler, the Parisian dreamer is not absolutely at
the mercy of the world he dreams:

> Insouciants et taciturnes,
> Des Ganges, dans le firmament,
> Versaient le trésor de leurs urnes
> Dans des gouffres de diamant.

>> Listless and taciturn,
>> the Ganges in the firmament
>> poured the treasure of their urns
>> in the diamond abysses.

> Architecte de mes féeries,
> Je faisais, à ma volonté,
> Sous un tunnel de pierreries
> Passer un océan dompté;

>> Architect of my fairy lands,
>> I let pass, as I wished,
>> under a tunnel of jewels
>> a subdued ocean;

> Et tout, même la couleur noire,
> Semblait fourbi, clair, irisé;
> Le liquide enchâssait sa gloire
> Dans le rayon cristallisé.

>> And everything, even the black color,
>> seemed burnished, clear, iridescent;
>> the liquid mounted (set, enshrined)
>> its glory in the crystallized ray.

> Nul astre d'ailleurs, nuls vestiges
> De soleil, même au bas du ciel,
> Pour illuminer ces prodiges,
> Qui brillaient d'un feu personnel!

>> Besides there were no stars, no
>> vestiges of the sun, even at the rim
>> of the sky, to light these prodigies,
>> which blazed in their fire!

Et sur ces mouvantes merveilles
Planait (terrible nouveauté!
Tout pour l'oeil, rien pour les oreilles!)
Un silence d'éternité.

> And over these shifting marvels
> hovered — terrible novelty! everything
> for the eye, nothing for the ears! —
> a silence of eternity.

When Baudelaire himself speaks of the close resemblance between Poe's poems and those he wrote, he allows for the differences in "temperament and climate." Rich and brilliant, Baudelaire's dream imagery is very different from that of Poe's poem. The sensuousness of Baudelaire does not altogether account for the difference. In other poems, Poe is also capable of brilliance, jeweled skies, crystal waters, labyrinths of light, and at least naiad airs; Baudelaire is capable of both *frissons de terreur* and dread of the dark abyss. In the dream landscapes they share the skies of fire and an irrefutable restlessness; each has an intensity and a clarity and a sense of vastness. Baudelaire's imagery is, however, *more* artificial, more reified, and less at the mercy of an indifferent nature. For Poe, nature speaks, as he said in *Al Aaraaf*, but nature is not for him as it was for Baudelaire "a temple whose living colonnades/ Breathe forth a mystic speech." Poe occasionally "describes" "violets that lie/ In myriad types of the human eye," but he rarely humanizes the earth. It is Baudelaire who, in other poems, figures "Nature once in lustful hot undress," "a young giantess," "a queen," and imagines himself "a voluptuous cat at her feet," or stretches her out across the plains and sleeps "in the shadow of her breasts at ease/ Like a small hamlet at a mountain's base." Accordingly, it is Baudelaire's dreamer who can channel and "let pass" as he wishes the ocean of his fairyland.

Baudelaire's poem concludes, as did Poe's, with an announcement of waking up. While Poe attends to the lonesome way by which the traveler wanders home, and simply mentions "home" as if it were of little interest in contrast to the place of the dreams, Baudelaire's dreamer quickly opens his eyes and attends briefly to the dull "everyday" existence in which he *is* enclosed by contrast with the exotic life of the dream:

En rouvrant mes yeux pleins de flamme
J'ai vu l'horreur de mon taudis,
Et senti, rentrant dans mon âme,
La pointe des soucis maudits;

> On reopening my eyes full of fire
> I saw the horror of my hovel,
> and felt, reentering my soul,
> the point of the cursed anxieties;

La pendule aux accents funèbres
Sonnait brutalement midi,
Et le ciel versait des ténèbres
Sur le triste monde engourdi.

> The pendulum with funereal accents
> sounded brutally midday,
> and the sky poured darkness
> on the sad, dull world.

Once upon a midday dreary Baudelaire read Poe and took him into the French imagination. Among the French poet's souvenirs of the American he understood so well are an old pendulum clock, anxieties, dull realities, and the dream of immense space. But the visualization of the space differs from that of Poe; without trees and heavy dews or the snows of the lily, without mountains or the murmur of rivers or dismal swamps and those amphibians that are as natural to them as to fairytales, the scene of "Rêve parisien" is not plagiarized from him. What Baudelaire did not quite share with Poe was the contemplation and conscious experience of an American landscape.

6

Poe was not a great nature poet. He did not, like Thoreau, live in the woods for two years and speak in the quickly recognized tone of authority about "the little fishy friend," the loon, leaf, and vegetable mould. Poe did not, like Mark Twain, know the great temperamental Mississippi River and its shores about which Huck Finn could write the homely, spontaneous poetry of being there. He did not, like Emily Dickinson, brag that "Several of nature's people I know/ And they know me." He did, however, share the romantic involvement with nature, and he was a solitary walker in the country, not in the London crowd.

The walks gave him, scavenger that he was, scenes for both the poetry and the prose. In the first poem, *Tamerlane,* the hero speaks of "roaming the forest, and the wild"; the mountain soil and the mists of Taglay belong to the state of Virginia. In "A Tale of the Ragged Mountains" (1844),

Bedloe takes lengthy rambles "among the chain of wild and dreary hills that lie westward and southward of Charlottesville." One walk is described directly:

> I bent my steps immediately to the mountains, and . . . entered a gorge which was entirely new to me. I followed the windings of this path with much interest. The scenery which presented itself on all sides, although scarcely entitled to be called grand, had about it an indescribable and to me a delicious aspect of dreary desolation. The solitude seemed absolutely virgin. I could not help believing that the green sods and gray rocks upon which I trod had been trodden never before by the foot of a human being. So entirely secluded, and in fact inaccessible, except through a series of accidents, is the entrance of the ravine, that it is by no means impossible that I was indeed the first adventurer . . . who had ever penetrated its recess. [H 5:166-67]

Poe scrambled over Sullivan's Island, near Charleston, S. C., and used the locale for "The Gold-Bug" (1843). "Morning on the Wissahiccon" (1844) is a sketch in praise of the little-known beauty of that stream and gorge north of Philadelphia as well as a reveling "in the visions of . . . ancient days . . . when the red man trod alone, with the elk, upon the ridges" above the river. A version of "Ulalume" (1847) was composed after a walk of a dozen miles from Fordham to Mamaroneck, N. Y. (M 411). A "pedestrian trip . . . through one or two of the river counties of New York" leads the walker to an ideal place, "Landor's Cottage" (1849).[19]

"The Island of the Fay" (1841), in which Poe is an exemplary walker, reveals the pleasure he took in being alone in the natural world. The essay, which is chronologically between "The Coliseum" (1833) and "Dream-Land" (1844), belongs to Poe's most productive and relatively secure period. A vision, a waking dream, of Poe's brief maturity, it is a fine moment in his evocation of the sense of place, a sequestered and silent island, leafed in the green foliage of summer and fragrant with the odors of an unknown shrub. Located in a stream amid a far distant region of mountain locked within mountain, the island is not a specifically identifiable place. Still, Poe's epigraph — "No place is without its local spirit" — is appropriately pointed when "The Island of the Fay" is compared with an island frequented by another solitary walker, Jean-Jacques Rousseau, whose account of an experience of the spirit of place precedes the American by more than half a century.

In *Les Rêveries d'un promeneur solitaire* (1782), Rousseau's sympathy with nature anticipates the romantic poets' interest in a subject which sustains writers as different as Wordsworth and Poe. The "Fifth Promenade"[20] is especially notable; it is also pertinent for an expression of sentiments realized in a landscape that is considered a European equivalent to American nature.

The setting for the fifth walk is the Isle of Saint-Pierre, in the middle of Lake Bienne. "This small island," Rousseau asserts, "is little known, even in Switzerland. No traveller, that I know of, has mentioned it." It is, however, "very agreeable, and exceptionally situated for the happiness of a man who likes to be alone." Rousseau declares himself such a man, "alone but not lonely." He then describes the region. The banks of the lake are

> more savage and romantic than those of Lake Geneva, because the rocks and the woods more closely border the water; but they are not less smiling. If there is less cultivation of the fields and vineyards, fewer towns and houses, there are also more natural vendure, more fields, shaded grove retreats, more frequent contrasts and undulations. . . . It is interesting for solitary contemplatives who love to intoxicate themselves at leisure with the charms of nature, and to recollect themselves in a silence which is troubled by no other noise than the cry of eagles, the broken chirping of some birds, and the rolling of the torrents which fall from the mountains. This beautiful pool, almost round in form, encloses in its midst two small islands, one inhabited and cultivated, about half a league around; the other smaller, deserted and fallow. . . .

This matter-of-fact, almost restrained, description hardly confirms the comment that the scene is savage or romantic; its proximity to less sparsely cultivated rural areas affords an escape from the usual traces of men and makes the island atypical. Rousseau, the social philosopher, does not refrain from considering the point that the use of the soil of the smaller island for the repair of natural damages to the larger one is like the use of the substance of the weak to profit the powerful. But it is not for such passages that the "Fifth Walk" is famous. They serve as a contrast with Rousseau's account of "what it was there attractive enough to excite" in his heart "regrets so vivid, so tender and so lasting, that after fifteen years" it is impossible for him "to think of this cherished habitation without feeling every time transported by the rush of desire."

Rousseau eases the reader into what it was:

> When the evening approached, I would descend the summits of the island and I would with pleasure sit down on the edge of the lake, on the beach, in some hidden retreat; there, the noise of the waves and the agitation of the water fixed my senses and chased from my soul all other agitation, [and] plunged her in a delicious revery,

where the night would surprise me often without my noticing it. The ebb and flow of this water, its continuing noise, but swollen by intervals, beating incessantly upon my ears and eyes, replaced the internal movements that the reveries would extinguish in me, and sufficed to make me feel with pleasure my existence, without bothering to think.

This modest passage depicts one of the great moments in the history of the human spirit. Giving himself freely to the pleasure of being in the place, Rousseau forgets everything, tensions, political and social issues, time itself. Letting himself be taken by the ambience and the sensuous rhythms of the water, he is simultaneously free to match his rhythms, his revery, his heart to the great heart of nature itself. The experience of being harmoniously and serenely alive and one with the landscape, of feeling without thinking, and without metaphysical anguish, but simply and fully accepting mortal existence: this is an august moment for solitary man. Here is both the absolute contemplation of a landscape in which it is hardly possible to be more at home and the imagination of a landscape which is neither distanced nor idealized but intimately experienced and cherished.

The integrity of the experience is naturally threatened:

> Now and again, would come to life some feeble and short reflections on the instability of things of this world, for which the surface of the waters offered me the image; but soon these light impressions were effaced in the uniformity of the continual movement which would lull me, and which, without any action of my soul, would never cease to bind me to the place so that called by the time and the signal [for an appointment] agreed upon, I could not tear myself away without effort.

Rousseau, however, is unwilling to forget the reality of the experience and its meaning for him:

> The happiness that my heart regrets does not at all consist of fugitive instants but a simple and permanent state, which has nothing vivid in itself, but whose lasting quality increases the charm to the point to find in it finally the supreme bliss.

Although the moment was of necessity "in time," and therefore could not be arrested, it paradoxically persisted "in time." Rousseau, meditating upon the reality, explains it at appropriate length. First, on the necessity of being "in time":

Everything is in a continual change on earth. Nothing keeps a constant and arrested form, and our feelings which are attached to exterior things pass and change necessarily like them. Always in front of us or behind us, they recall the past which is no longer or foresee the future which often will not come to be; there is nothing solid there to which the heart can attach itself. Therefore one has on earth hardly any other pleasure than the ones that pass; for the happiness that lasts, I doubt that it is known. Hardly is there in our most vivid joys, an instant when the heart is truly able to say to us: *I wish that this moment would last forever.* And how can one call happiness a fugitive state which still leaves the heart unquiet and empty, which makes us regret something before, or desire still something after?

Rousseau then explains in one long ecstatic breath the paradoxically permanent moment:

If there is a state where the soul finds a ground solid enough to rest there completely and reassemble all his being, without need to recall the past or to run on into the future, where time doesn't exist for her [the soul], where the present lasts forever, without for all that marking its duration and without any trace of succession, without any other feeling of privation or of joy, of pleasure or of pain, of desire or of fear, without any other feeling than that of our existence, and that that feeling alone can fill the soul completely: so long as that state lasts, the one who finds himself in it can call himself happy, not with an imperfect, poor and relative happiness, such as one finds in the pleasure of life, but a happiness sufficient, perfect and full, which leaves the soul no emptiness that she feels the need to fill.

Such was the state Rousseau says he found himself in during the solitary revery on the island of Saint-Pierre.

Rousseau's is not a daydream in which he loses himself, but the visionary experience of finding himself in nature. He is almost negligent in describing the scene; had it been as savage and romantic as he claimed, Rousseau would hardly have been so magnificently able to discover himself there. After a few cursory remarks about either lying in a boat that he would let drift willy-nilly in the water, or sitting on the lake, river, or brook, Rousseau asks, what does one enjoy in such a situation?

Nothing exterior to oneself, nothing if not oneself and one's own existence: as long as this state lasts, one is sufficient to oneself, like God. The sentiment of existence devoid of all other feeling is in itself a precious feeling of contentment and peace, which suffice alone to make this existence dear and sweet to him who would know how to divest himself of all sensual and mundane impressions that come incessantly to distract us and trouble the sweetness here on earth.

The American writer was not apt to have such an experience in nature. Bryant, in "A Forest Hymn," communed with God. Thoreau, whose life was "deepened and clarified" at Walden Pond, came perhaps closest to it; he wanted to experience the eternal present, but he was much too strenuous, much too given to self-contemplation and conscious self-dramatization in the practice of nature's lessons to be able to feel instantaneously the pleasure of existence. Whitman, on the other hand, knew the peace and sweetness of being. He affirms in "Song of Myself" the experience of loafing on the grass one transparent summer morning and realizing, physically, the union of soul and body. But he feels "the puzzle of puzzles/ And that we call being." The silence at the center of that dynamic poem is followed by the question, "To be in any form, what is that?/ (Round and round we go, all of us, and ever come back thither). . . ." Poe's is a vision of the polarities of being and non-being.

In "The Island of the Fay" (H 4:193-99) Poe recounts an experience of revery as evening approaches in the solitude of nature.[21] Whether Poe knew the *Rêveries* or not, he cites Rousseau in other connections, and follows the French romantic in praise of retreats to nature: "There is one pleasure still within the reach of fallen mortality and perhaps only one – which owes even more than does music to the accessory sentiment of seclusion. I mean the happiness experienced in the contemplation of natural scenery." Poe's orientation is immediately different from that of Rousseau, from whom nothing was heard about "fallen mortality." Yet, like Rousseau, Poe values being alone in nature: the man who would see "aright the glory of God upon the earth must in solitude behold that glory." He insists that "the presence – not of human life only, but of life in any other form than that of the green things which grow upon the soil and are voiceless – is a stain upon the landscape – is at war with the genius of the scene." Poe, then, seems as qualified as Rousseau to intoxicate himself with the charms of a natural scene; but, in contrast to the European, he is already much more a beholder, an onlooker, than a participant. Poe writes:

I love, indeed, to regard the dark valleys, and the gray rocks, and the waters that silently smile, and the forests that sigh in uneasy slumbers, and the proud watchful mountains that look down upon all, –

> I love to regard these as themselves but the colossal members of one
> vast animate and sentient whole —

"To regard these as themselves" risks separating oneself from their life.
The perspective, too, recalls that of Poe's poem "The Coliseum": the
pilgrim is separated from the ruins and is quietly down under "the colossal
members" of the vast structure and the sentient stones.

But nature is as alive for Poe as it is for Rousseau. Poe proposes that
the endowment of matter with vitality is the "leading" principle in the
operation of God: "As we find cycle within cycle without end — yet all
revolving around one far-distant centre which is the God-head, may we not
analogically suppose, in the same manner, life within life, the less within
the greater, and all within the Spirit Divine?" Poe's universe is magnificently conceived. His conception of it is turned, however, toward the
humbling of man who errs, through self-esteem, if he believes himself of
more moment than the "vast 'clod of the valley' " to which he denies a
soul because "he does not behold it." Poe argues that "it is scarcely logical
to imagine" God's leading principle confined "to regions of the minute,
where we daily trace it, and not extending to those of the august." Such
ideas, such "fancies," Poe comments, "have always given to my medita-
tions among the mountains, and the forests, by the rivers and the ocean,"
a tinge of the fantastic. Not only speculating, he is carefully preparing for
the revery to follow. The retreat to nature is not, as with Rousseau, for
recollecting and finding one's self. Poe's revery will not be in a rush of
desire, like Rousseau's, to match the rhythms of the heart to the life of
nature, and to dream "I feel; therefore, I am." Poe's "matter endowed
with vitality" anticipates the appearance of a fay.

Poe must reiterate that he qualifies as a man responsive to nature:

> My wanderings amid such scenes have been many, and far-search-
> ing, and often solitary; and the interest with which I have strayed
> through many a dim deep valley, or gazed into the reflected Heaven
> of many a bright lake, has been an interest greatly deepened by the
> thought that I have strayed and gazed *alone*.

During one of these "lonely journeyings, amid a far-distant region of
mountain locked within mountain, and sad rivers and melancholy tarns
writhing or sleeping within all," he chances upon a rivulet and island which
by design he does not name. The time is "the leafy June," and he throws
himself on the turf beneath the branches of an unknown shrub as he
contemplates the scene. There is no suggestion that the sequestered island
is like Rousseau's "exceptionally situated" in the sense that it contrasts

with nearby towns, houses, cultivated fields, and vineyards. For all Poe's wanderings, he has never been there before and will probably never come there again. One does not feel that there is any likelihood of the American's being able to speak of the place as "a cherished habitation." The setting may be congenial to Poe's temperament — "sad rivers and melancholy tarns" are supposed to be his scene — and his description may be for no other purpose than to foreshadow the vision of the fay. Is it not also possible that, given Poe's receptiveness, the landscape evokes the fancy? Poe feels both an ease and "interest" in the place, but he is not altogether at home there.

Poe's is clearly to be a divided vision. The oppositions are at first only intimated:

> On all sides — save to the west, where the sun was about sinking — arose the verdant walls of the forest. The little river which turned sharply in its course, and was thus immediately lost to sight, seemed to have no exit from its prison, but to be absorbed by the deep green foliage of the trees to the east — while in the opposite quarter . . . there poured down noiselessly and continuously into the valley, a rich golden and crimson water-fall from the sunset fountains of the sky.

About midway in the short vista a small circular island lay upon the stream. The very green and abundant vegetation, the afternoon shadows, the bank, and the mirror-like water so blended that "it was scarcely possible to say at what point upon the slope of the emerald turf" the "crystal domination" of the water began. Holding in view both the eastern and western extremities of the island, Poe observes the marked difference between them. In an ambience of light:

> The latter was all one radiant harem of garden beauties. It glowed and blushed beneath the eyes of the slant sunlight, and fairly laughed with flowers. The grass was short, springy, sweet-scented, and Asphodel-interspersed. The trees were lithe, mirthful, erect — bright, slender, and graceful, — of eastern figure and foliage, with bark smooth, glossy, and parti-colored. There seemed a deep sense of life and joy about it all; and although no airs blew from out the heavens, yet everything had motion through the gentle sweepings to and fro of innumerable butterflies, that might have been mistaken for tulips with wings.

Poe approaches Baudelaire's exotic imagery of nature; there is a muted sensuousness, and the scene is ever so slightly although not voluptuously humanized. The place is neither macabre nor without its charms. The description of butterflies "that might have been mistaken for tulips with wings" is less effective than that in Poe's early poem "Fairy-Land" (1829), which ends with images of a moon's atomies dissevering into a shower "Of which those butterflies,/ Of Earth, who seek the skies,/ And so come down again/ (Never contented things!)/ Have brought a specimen/ Upon their quivering wings . . . . " (M 141). Since elusive light does not dominate Poe's visual imagination and is rarely noticed as one of his qualities, attention has been primarily on "the power of blackness" which has been synonymous with the solitary Poe. And it is toward darkness that Poe turns:

> The other or eastern end of the isle was whelmed in the blackest shade. A sombre, yet beautiful and peaceful gloom here pervaded all things. The trees were dark in color and mournful in form and attitude — wreathing themselves into sad, solemn, and spectral shapes that conveyed ideas of mortal sorrow and untimely death. The grass wore the deep tint of the cypress, and the heads of its blades hung droopingly, and hither and thither among it were many small unsightly hillocks, low and narrow, and not very long, that had the aspects of graves, but were not; although over and all about them the rue and the rosemary clambered. The shade of the trees fell heavily upon the water, and seemed to bury itself therein, impregnating the depths of the element with darkness.

Then the divided vision is terminated:

> I fancied that each shadow, as the sun descended lower and lower, separated itself sullenly from the trunk that gave it birth, and thus became absorbed by the stream; while other shadows issued momently from the trees, taking the place of their predecessors thus entombed.

His fancy excited by the idea, Poe states that he "lost" himself in revery. Although it is tinged with the fantastic, Poe's revery is never out of time and is still within the place. Letting himself go, not with Rousseau's easy abandon to being alive but in response to the scene, Poe imagines that the island is the enchanted "haunt of the few gentle Fays who remain from the wreck of the race." Delicately echoing the belief in "fallen mortality," Poe does more than play with the sounds of enchanted-haunted. For him, the dying of the day becomes a vision of the dying of the year, and the fancy of the fays' "yielding up their sweet lives," an allegory of human existence. The fays are not identified with the wreck of the race; their lives are sweet; they are doomed in time; the enchanted land is not the villain of the piece. But Poe is not for a moment able to find, like Rousseau, the consolation of feeling and fully accepting "the sweetness here on earth."

The theme of cyclical renewal and the contrary theme of recurrent death, which the fays symbolize, are augmented in the serpentine rhythms of Poe's prose:

> While the sun sank rapidly to rest, and eddying currents careered round and round the island, bearing upon their bosom large, dazzling, white flakes of the bark of the sycamore — flakes which, in their multiform positions upon the water, a quick imagination might have converted into anything it pleased, — while I thus mused, it appeared to me that the form of one of those very Fays about whom I had been pondering, made its way slowly into darkness from out the light at the western end of the island. She stood erect in a singularly fragile canoe, and urged it with the mere phantom of an oar. While within the influence of the lingering sunbeams, her attitude seemed indicative of joy — but sorrow deformed it as she passed within the shade. Slowly she glided along, and at length rounded the islet and re-entered the region of light. "The revolution which has just been made by the Fay," continued I, musingly, "is the cycle of the brief year of her life. She has floated through her winter and through her summer. She is a year nearer unto Death; for I did not fail to see that, as she came into the shade, her shadow fell from her, and was swallowed up in the dark water, making its blackness more than black."

Again and again and again the boat appears and the Fay makes the circuit of the island. Floating from the light into the gloom, she grows fainter and more indistinct, her joy diminishes, her care and uncertainty increase; darker shadows fall from her and the gloom deepens. Then, at length:

> When the sun had utterly departed, the Fay, now the mere ghost of her former self, went disconsolately with her boat into the region of the ebony flood and that she issued thence at all I cannot say, for darkness fell over all things and I beheld her magical figure no more.

Poe has almost forgotten "the glory of God" upon earth. In spite of the experience of happiness in the momentary illumination, the final mood is one of emptiness, and loss: "I beheld her magical figure no more" is a frail remembrance. In spite of the nuances of the fancy, Poe is not sustained but regretful.

If it seems that Poe has capitulated to the influence of Thomas Moore's

"Ballad of the Dismal Swamp," Poe's fancy is not nearly as comforting as Moore's. The Irish poet, a summer visitor, could change fireflies into lamps and easily reunite romantic lovers in a nearly uninhabitable landscape; Poe, who roamed the land in all seasons for many years, transformed the joy in meditating upon it into a fancy that allegorizes sentient, transient life and the increment of sorrow.

Perhaps the transformation is merely a consequence of Poe's personal imagination, a limited, exhausted imagination. Almost everything Poe experienced, it has been customarily believed, was touched from the beginning with death. Perhaps the fancy has little to do with the landscape itself. Rousseau, it can be argued, was always more vigorous and had one last burst of energy when he wrote *Les Rêveries.* He was able to stand up to God himself. Rousseau's was a strong heart. Poe was heartsick. The energy, charm, and radiance of the poetic moments in "The Island of the Fay," nevertheless, reveal an independent, pensive man standing alone and time-bound in God's nature. Poe was not only capable of poise and composure in solitary meditation upon mortal life in the heart of the great, silent American landscape; he was also capable of transcending the solitude by means of an imaginative, if fanciful, allegory of "The Island of the Fay."

Poe's ideal man is Ellison in "The Domain of Arnheim" (1847). Ellison travels for several years with a friend in search of a suitable place to build a house (H 4:176-96). Ellison wishes a locality that will offer "the composure but not the depression of solitude." A thousand spots with which the friend is enraptured are rejected without hesitation by Ellison for the reason, of which the friend must be convinced, that vast and spectacular landscapes are not necessarily sustaining. "We came at length," the friend says, "to an elevated tableland of wonderful fertility and beauty." It afforded a panoramic prospect very little less in extent than that of Aetna, and in Ellison's opinion, as well as that of the friend, surpassed "the far-famed view from that mountain in all the true elements of the picturesque." The view is of a great American landscape. Ellison draws a sigh of deep delight after gazing entranced for nearly an hour on the scene. He finally speaks:

> I am aware, . . . I know that here, in my circumstances, nine-tenths of the most fastidious of men would rest content. This panorama is indeed glorious, and I should rejoice in it but for the excess of its glory. The taste of all the architects I have ever known leads them, for the sake of "prospect," to put up buildings on hilltops. The error is obvious. Grandeur in any of its moods, but especially in that of extent, startles, excites — and then fatigues, depresses. For the occasional scene nothing can be better — for the constant

view nothing worse.

Poe is writing, not like a great nature poet but like a connoisseur of landscape. Ellison continues the analysis of "natural taste":

> And, in the constant view, the most objectionable phase of grandeur is that of extent; the worst phase of extent, that of distance. It is at war with the sentiment and with the sense of *seclusion* — the sentiment and sense which we seek to humor in "retiring to the country." In looking from the summit of a mountain we cannot help feeling *abroad* in the world. The heart-sick avoid distant prospects as a pestilence.

Ellison's spoofing of "the heart-sick" may reflect one of Poe's wryly humorous and self-critical moments. But Poe did not avoid American prospects. He contemplated them absolutely and boldly; he distanced and transported them to ancient ruins; he dreamed them; he tried to humanize them; he even let imagination turn to fancy and allegory in the island solitude of a great landscape. Grandeur startles, excites — and then fatigues, depresses. No wonder that Poe was also interested in the vogue for landscape gardening.[22]

7

What any writer, including Poe, has to say about man's place in nature depends in part upon the landscape that, as he wrote in "The Lake," it is his lot to haunt. Any writer, anywhere, may come to the conclusions that mortal existence is fragile, that there is an inexorable isolation at the heart of the human community, and that man is doomed by his own frailty, whether nature is cultivated or wild, sympathetic or indifferent. But the reaches of uninhabited and untenanted space account, as tellingly as Poe's aesthetic theory or alienated temperament, for his characteristically empty landscapes in comparison with landscapes of writers whose locale made images of emptiness atypical. Poe's aesthetic, predicated in *Al Aaraaf*, neither denied nor abhorred the phenomenal world as the realm in which the poet is an introspective voyager. Young Angelo, the one man transported to the celestial realm of Al Aaraaf, turned his dark eye trembling toward the orb of Earth as he sat talking with Ianthe, the spirit he loved. Recalling the beauty of the world he left — the proud temple and columned walls of the Parthenon, one-half the garden of the globe, and the tenantless cities of the desert — he confessed that he "half . . . wish'd to be again of men" (lines 194-226). The reciprocity between Poe's temperament and his sense of a great landscape gives his poetry and prose the peculiar, desolate, intense qualities that have caused many readers to think the thrust of his work was toward repudiation of the earth. To attend to the relation between the subjective ideality and the given reality on which that ideality depends does not vitiate Poe's worth, but rather strengthens appreciation of the power of his art and its reliance on an American experience.

Poe's encounter with obstinate distances is no more clearly expressed in any of his work than in a trio of poems that span two decades of his brief career following *Al Aaraaf*. The poems reveal the slender attitudes, the longing and nostalgia typical of Poe's peregrinations within his own country. Death permeates, or essays to dominate, or casts its shadow on the landscape. And in one of them, "Eldorado" (M 463), the journey encompasses the joys and sorrows of the search for an ideal world that will be realized only in an ascent to the high plateaus of the moon and a descent into the valley of the shadow [of death]. The images of ideality itself are the images of earth.

The poems "The Valley of Unrest" (1831, 1845) and "The City in the Sea" (1831, 1845) depend upon and evoke a sense of time and space. The first is structured by the contrast of a remembered "once" and "now." In the second the monuments of the city are "Time-eaten." The visions are of distant landscapes within the perimeters of global space. The scenes are far away in relation to the accustomed locus of the observer, and they are distant from one another — in the first version of "The Valley of Unrest" the place is far away within the golden east; the city in the second poem lies alone far down within the dim west (M 189-204).

The people of the valley have gone to "the wars." It is as if the place has no other human history; in the final version of the poem, there are no signs of human habitation and no names. The people trusted to beneficent nature to keep watch over the valley; but the ambience of all things lovely was short-lived. Nature itself has become preternaturally restless; the sorrow of the deserted valley is expressed by brooding airs, weeping flowers, eternal dews, and perennial change: a terrible beauty is born in the solitude. Although the mood is elegiac, there is no consolation to counter the irredeemable golden vision of the silent past; the present is a succession of moments of unquiet grief, for which the visitor to the scene shall confess and by implication atone. The delicacy and mystery of the manifestations of sorrow are attributable to neither the traditions of the sublime nor of the picturesque. The poem belongs, rather, to the American experience of the lost Eden and the restive spirit.

"The City in the Sea" is death's other kingdom. The melancholy waters that encircle the town are resigned to having been forgotten: they share with the long-forgotten bowers of the city the stagnation, silence, hideous serenity, and garish light of the tenebrific scene. There is no living human presence — "the good and the bad and the worst and the best/ Have gone to their eternal rest." The sole inhabitant of the city is gigantic Death, whose proud tower among the architectural ruins dominates the geography of the dead. Although the architecture is said to resemble "nothing that is ours," it is seen as facade; and although no one could live or visit there, the pictorial lines of force in the description of the scene center on etchings of "the viol, the violet, and the vine" that grace the friezes of once mortal shrines. The art, the idols, the riches, the jewels of humankind, however, are powerless to hasten a change in the natural phenomena; the forces of nature itself effect the only action in the poem — the progression from silence and stasis to faint sounds and feeble motion as the desolate city sinks gradually into the sea. Legends of lost cities, the American West, and the Dismal Swamp, as well as literary sources, have been cited as influences in Poe's poem.[23] "The City in the Sea" shares with "The Valley of Unrest" a vision of the relation between man and nature; counterchanging the poignant theme of lost beatitude in a natural setting, the theme intimated in the depiction of the deserted city is the opposition of nature to immobility and the hideous serenity of Death. There is no promise of restoration or human exaltation. On the contrary, Hell shall rise up and do reverence to the engulfed town which leaves a void within the sky, "the filmy Heaven." The poem is one of the most comfortless in nineteenth-century American literature, and even though the new world was one to which, as the cliché had it, "the worst and the best" of Europe came, the experience only intensified the realization of what Melville called the harborless immensities where time stops and is never ending.

The enclosed space and the catastrophic life for which Poe provided images,[24] especially in the psychological inquiries of the fiction, are much less frequent in the poetry. The open landscape of one of the last poems, "Eldorado" (1849), has the lonely air but nothing that signals the trauma said to be so characteristic of Poe's perceptions of reality. The spur of the poem is the pleasure of the lone traveler who rides boldly in search of the ideal place — "the vague quest," as critics have called it. The sense of great distance traversed by the knight in sunshine and in shadow is conveyed by the sense of passing time. The play of "shadow" — first over the heart of the traveler grown old, and then in the encounter with a pilgrim shadow (like Eliot's "familiar compound ghost . . . intimate and unidentifiable," the "spirit unappeased and peregrine") — is not the play of the haunted palace and the conqueror worm. The easy cadences of the poem in which the knight rides and sings are hardly changed by the subtle halting of the rhythmic movement or the break in the rhyme when the pilgrim shadow, answering the knight's inquiry, encourages continuation of the journey "Over the Mountains/ Of the Moon,/ Down the Valley of the Shadow. . . ." The resonant verbal music and the harmonic resolution in the rhymes of the closing words

> "Ride, boldly ride,"
> The shade replied, —
> If you seek for Eldorado!"

lyrically affirm the high ironic, calm acceptance of the vast lonely terrain by the quixotic fellows in this Grand Canyon suite. The poem is not a great poem; nor is it a great moment in the history of the American spirit. But it is a good poem, and the idealization of the light-hearted quester — the simple language matching the simple theme of the romantic search for the ideal — in the poem serves well as a testament to Poe's spirit in the encounter with the empty spaces that are taken for granted in the American sublime. The extension of space is taken so much for granted, it goes almost without notice in such a poem as "Eldorado."

The subtleties of Poe's response to landscape in which there was a beauty based on emptiness or a lack of human dominion have never been thought equal to the acuteness of his perceptions of disordered states of mind. Since reality — according to Poe — was viewed from within, the ambience of the great solitary landscape that he knew and the characteristics of mania that he depicted have tempted readers to suppose that all his ingenuities were studies of his own aberrant consciousness. How could we account otherwise for the unwonted knowledge of the extreme states of suffering (isolated consciousness) to which he gave imaginary voices?

MERE HOUSEHOLD EVENTS
The Metaphysics of Mania

.

"*Some readers may think the conduct of the younger Wieland impossible. In support of its possibility the writer must appeal to physicians, and to men conversant with the latent springs and occasional perversions of the human mind.*"

Charles Brockden Brown, "Advertisement,"
Wieland

"*There are moments, when, even to the sober eye of Reason, the world of our sad humanity must assume the aspect of Hell; but the Imagination of Man is no Carathis [whose great object was to obtain favour with the powers of Darkness] to explore with impunity its every cavern. Alas! the grim legion of sepulchral terrors cannot be regarded as altogether fanciful; but like the Demons in whose company Afrasiah made his voyage down the Oxus, they must sleep, or they will devour us—they must be suffered to slumber, or we perish.*"

Poe, "Marginalia"

1

"My immediate purpose," Poe's narrator for "The Black Cat" (1842) writes, "is to place before the world, plainly, succinctly, and without comment, a series of mere household events" (H 5:143). The events, he continues, "have terrified — have tortured — have destroyed me." Neither expecting nor soliciting belief for "the most wild yet most homely narrative" he is about to pen, the narrator unburdens his soul — the story of the radical alteration in the temperament and character of a man "through the instrumentality of the Fiend Intemperance. . . . For what disease is like Alcohol!"

Poe's frequent use of a narrator who confesses some terrible personal history has always stimulated interest in the relation between life and work, especially on the part of readers inclined to forget that fiction is fiction. When Baudelaire, in the draft of a preface for *Les Fleurs du mal,* complained, "Every sin, every crime I have related has been imputed to me," he might have noted that Poe could have said the same thing. Is Poe himself, one can hardly help asking, confessing "mere household events" when a narrator reveals a history of radical alteration in temperament and character, a history that has terrified, tortured, and destroyed him? What, in a story such as "The Black Cat," is autobiographical, what is fictional? What gives the fiction — "The Fall of the House of Usher" or "The Tell-Tale Heart" or "The Pit and the Pendulum" — its impressive authority?

Explanations for the achievement are entangled in theories of the relation between the conscious and the unconscious as well as the influence of literary conventions and cultural history in the work.[1] Or there is the philosophical overview: Poe's great subject, the disintegration of the personality, culminates in the cosmology of *Eureka*, which postulates that "In the Original Unity of the First Thing Lies the Secondary Cause of All Things, with the Germ of Their Inevitable Annihilation."[2] Seen as an aesthetic whole, the work is thought to be consistent in theme and coherent in structure — the design for which (as T. S. Eliot said of a study of his literary criticism) was sketched out at the beginning of his career, and for which he spent the rest of his life filling in the details.

There are, however, parts of the design that do not stay in place. For Poe, like Eliot's ordinary man, experience was chaotic, irregular, fragmentary; our documents for studying the connections between that experience and the literature are incomplete. There were, we know, household events that gave vitality to the imagination of disaster with which Poe is identified. There were also applicable resources, medical texts, to give authority to the blood-curdling stories of mad hero-villains who maim, kill, and confess their deeds. In the Enlightenment spirit of institutional reform or concern with the treatment of criminals and the mentally ill, American and European doctors published studies of "moral insanity," diseases of the brain, and mania. These sources, together with the circumstances, epiphenomena, and pressures of Poe's mundane, ragged existence, permit us to trace his development as a writer of psychological insight.

When the narrator of "The Black Cat" speaks of the "Fiend Intemperance," he uses the old language of morality and religion; when he exclaims, "What disease is like Alcohol!" he uses a medical term. The reference to "instrumentality" relies on a theory of alcohol as agent, but is "the agent" caused or the cause? How did Poe and his contemporaries conceive of "alcoholism"? What did Poe know about himself, mental illness, and psychological disturbances — "the metaphysics of mania," a recurrent, if not obsessive subject in the stories? Is there, finally, conscious use of that knowledge in the fiction?

2

Since there is considerable information on the history of Poe's drinking in his letters as well as accounts by people who were associated with him, it is possible to take that material as an index of his view of alcoholism in relation to current medical studies of "mania." Although much of the material is well known, having been frequently cited, the evidence can bear further examination for the changes it reveals in Poe's perceptions of his psychobiographic history and in his self-knowledge.

The one period of his life for which there is verifiable information about Poe's drinking patterns is the Richmond period when Poe held his first job since he had served in the United States Army. Poe's letters, checked against other sources of information, especially letters of his employer, are at variance with the latter in the description of the job, for instance, but show no discrepancy in regard to the facts either reported or implied when drinking is the issue. If not untrustworthy in accounts he gave of the difficulties with drinking, the letters show further that Poe had little conscious understanding of himself in the uncertain beginning of his career as a writer.

During the early part of August 1835, Poe came from Baltimore to Richmond where he was to work on the *Southern Literary Messenger*, for which Thomas W. White was publisher. A letter from White to Lucian Minor, a Virginia lawyer, whose editorial services White sought and whose advice he received frequently, is dated August 18: "Mr. Poe is here also. — He tarries one month — and will aid all that lies in his power."[3] But Poe wrote on August 20 from Richmond to his brother, William Poe: "I have lately obtained the Editorship of the Southern Messenger" (O 1:68).

Poe also wrote on August 29 to Maria Clemm, the aunt in whose house he had lived in Baltimore. Asserting in the long letter that he has no wish to live, Poe explained the crisis straightway:

> Al[l] my thoughts are occupied with the supposition that both you & she [Virginia, Poe's future wife] will prefer to go with N. [eilson] Poe; I do sincerely believe that your *comforts* will for the present be secured — I cannot speak as regards your peace — your happiness. . . . It is useless to disguise the truth when Virginia goes with N. P. that I shall never behold her again — that is absolutely sure. . . . It is useless to expect advice forom[sic] me — what can I say? — can I, in honor & truth say — Virginia! do not go! do not go where you can be comfortable and perhaps happy — and on the other hand can I calmly resign my — life itself. If she had truly loved me would she not have rejected the offer with scorn? Oh God have mercy on me! If she goes with N. P. what are you to do, my own Aunty? [Then Poe mentioned the "dreams" he had had of getting a house and a garden and calling Virginia his wife, although] the situation has this morning been conferred upon another. Branch T. Saunders. but White has engaged to make my salary $60. a month, and we could live in comparative comfort & happiness. (O 1:69-71)

Anxious and self-pitying, Poe lamented that he was alone among strangers with not a soul to love him, promised that if the Clemms came to Richmond they would have better opportunities of entering into society where everyone received him with open arms, reprimanded Mrs. Clemm for the "worldly" tone in which she wrote, and offered her more than he had to offer. Finally, after asking whether she thought anyone could love Virginia more dearly than he, Poe requested that the decision be left to her: "Let me have, under her own hand, a letter bidding me *good-bye* — forever — and I [m]ay die — my heart will break — but I will say no more."

On September 4 Poe wrote to John Neal, critic and editor, and sent him a copy of the *Messenger*, "a magazine of which I have lately obtained the Editorship" (O 1:72). White, however, wrote to Minor on September 8:

> I am now as it were my own editor — No. 12 [the issue for August] is made out of my wits. When we meet, I will tell you why I was obliged to part with Sparhawk. Poe is now in my employ — not as Editor. He is unfortunately rather dissipated — and therefore I can place very little reliance upon him. His disposition is quite amiable. He will be some assistance to me in proofreading — at least I hope so. [J 1:98]

White also sent Minor a list of the contributors for the August number. "All the Critical and Literary Notices" were, White said, "by Mr. Poe." Poe's needs and abilities were obviously in conflict with White's faith in him. He was twenty-six years old; and White's was the first reference to Poe's being "dissipated."

Poe would later confirm White's note on the intemperance, but for the time being Poe concentrated baffled attention on the emotional crisis he was experiencing. He showed no awareness of medical theories connecting "dissipation" with mental disturbance; the language in which he described the disturbance predates that of early nineteenth-century medicine, and derives from either literature or eighteenth-century "psychiatry."[4] Poe wrote about himself on September 11 to John P. Kennedy, the Baltimore lawyer and author who aided him. Expressing a "deep sense of gratitude" for Kennedy's "frequent and effectual assistance and kindness," Poe reported:

> Through your influence Mr. White has been induced to employ me in assisting him with the editorial duties at a salary of $520 per annum. The situation is agreeable to me for many reasons — but alas! it appears to me that nothing can now give me pleasure — or the slightest gratification. . . . I am suffering under a depression of spirits such as I have never felt before. I have struggled in vain against the influence of this melancholy — *You will believe me* when I say that I am miserable in spite of the great improvement in my circumstances. . . . I am wretched and know not why. . . . Con-

vince me that it is worth one's while – that it is at all necessary to live. . . . Persuade me to do what is right. . . . oh pity me! for I feel that my words are incoherent – but I will recover myself. You will not fail to see that I am suffering under a depression of spirits which will not fail to ruin me should it be long continued. . . . Urge me to do what is right. . . . [O 1:73-74]

One can surmise that Poe was cagily playing with the phrase " a depression of spirits," but "the influence of this melancholy" and the fear of incoherence left no doubt that he was emotionally in need of help. He also saw the need in relation to moral choice or conduct. A postscript stated that Mr. White desired Poe to ask Kennedy for a contribution to the magazine.

White's correspondence verified Poe's report of his psychological state, and did not speculate on reasons for either his drinking or his despair. In a letter, again to Minor, White wrote on September 21: "Poe has flew the track already. His habits were not good. – He is in addition the victim of melancholy. I should not be at all astonished to hear that he had been guilty of suicide. I am now alone" (J 1:100). White had no magazine for October and November. Poe had returned to Baltimore. On September 22 he took out a license for marriage to Virginia Clemm. Having checked all the evidence possible, Arthur Hobson Quinn thinks the story that Poe and Virginia were married rests on rumor, whereas Thomas Ollive Mabbott finds the evidence somewhat incomplete and is "convinced that Poe and Virginia were privately married."[5] Early in October, however, Poe brought Mrs. Clemm and Virginia to Richmond.

White had written to Poe on September 29:

Dear Edgar,
. . . That you are sincere in all your promises, I firmly believe. But, Edgar, when you once again tread these streets, I have my fears that your resolves would fall through, – and that you would again sip the juice even though it stole away your sense. Rely on your strength, and you are gone! Look to your Maker for help, and you are safe!. . .

You have fine talents, Edgar, – and you ought to have them respected as well as yourself. Learn to respect yourself, and you will very soon find that you are respected. Separate yourself from the bottle, and bottle companions, for ever!

Tell me if you can and will do so – and let me hear that it is your fixed purpose never to yield to temptation.

If you should come to Richmond again, and again should be an assistant in my office, it must be expressly understood by us that all engagements on my part would be dissolved, the moment you get drunk.

> No man is safe who drinks before breakfast! No man can do so, and attend to business properly. . . . [H 17:21]

Poe was back at work at least by October 8 when he wrote at the request of White to Robert M. Bird, the dramatist, to solicit aid in occasional or regular contributions to the *Messenger* (O 1:75).

White wrote on October 20, 1835, to Minor, sent a proof-sheet of an address by Minor, and reported that "Mr. Poe, who is with me again, read it over by copy with great care. He is very much pleased with it – in fact he passes great encomiums on it. . . " (J 1:102-3). White wrote again, four days later, to Minor and asked for a modest paragraph mentioning that E. V. Sparhawk, who had been announced as White's assistant in the May issue of the magazine, retired from its editorship with the July number (J 1:104). Minor was also to announce that the paper was under White's editorial management "assisted by several gentlemen of distinguished literary attainments." The notice was a delicate matter. White said: "You may introduce Mr. Poe's name as amongst those engaged to contribute to its columns – taking care not to say as editor. All this I wish you to manage with great care for me. Let it come in a separate letter to me – directed to 'T. W. White.' " Minor's announcement appeared in the December issue.

White sent Minor, on December 25, a list of the writers for the January 1836 number: "All the Critical Notices are from the pen of Poe – who I rejoice to tell you keeps from the Bottle." The critical notices numbered sixteen pages (J 1:107).

Poe wrote on January 22 to Kennedy to thank him for a "kind letter of advice of some months ago" (O 1:81). Poe said:

> It was not without great influence upon me. I have, since then, fought the enemy manfully, and am now in every respect, comfortable and happy. I know you will be *pleased* to hear this. My health is better than for years past, my mind fully occupied, my pecuniary difficulties have vanished, I have a fair prospect of future success – in a word all is right.

Poe then expressed gratitude to Kennedy without whose "timely aid" it would not have been possible to bear the trials he had undergone, and gave Kennedy "a great degree" of the credit for the present happiness. Poe reported that White was liberal and paid him for extra work, that friends in Richmond had received him with open arms, and that his reputation was extending. "Contrast all this," Poe concluded, "with those circumstances of absolute despair in which you found me, and you will see how great reason I have to be grateful to God — and to yourself." Kennedy's reply on February 9 included the advice: "Be rigidly temperate both in body and mind" (H 17:29).

It is clear that White's letters corroborate Poe's account of his difficulties with "the enemy," alcohol. In neither account is there the slightest conjecture about connections between the crisis in Poe's "family" life, his melancholy, and his intemperance.

There is no evidence of Poe's failing to meet his job responsibilities or of his drinking for almost a year after his return to work in early October of 1835. Poe's success in improving both the quality and circulation of the *Messenger* during the year is well known. "All," however, was not as "fair" for him as he said it was on January 22, 1836, when he wrote to thank Kennedy. There is, for instance, a January 26 letter from Nathaniel Beverley Tucker, novelist and professor of law at William and Mary College, to White: ". . . Last night I received a letter from Mr. Poe by which I learn that you may not feel as much confidence in his capacity for the duties of his station as is necessary for your mutual comfort."[6] (Tucker also wrote to Poe and advised him freely.) When White accepted Poe as editor is not clear, but not until August 25 was there a letter indicating White's willingness to describe accurately the job Poe was doing. White wrote to William Scott, proprietor of the *New York Weekly Messenger*: "Courtesy to Mr. Poe whom I employ to edit my paper makes it a matter of etiquette with me to submit all articles intended for the Messenger to his judgment and I abide by his dicta." If White held to the terms of Poe's employment in September of the year before, this letter must mean that Poe had kept "from the bottle" (O 1:72). There were, nevertheless, other difficulties between White and the young editor.

One of the difficulties was over editorial policy and practices. When White's new assistant returned to Baltimore, White wrote on October 1 to Minor to ask whether he thought Poe had been unnecessarily severe in "well penned and witty" but sarcastic remarks about James Fenimore Cooper (J 1:101-2). No more is heard about this kind of problem for over a year. Then White in a letter of December 27, 1836, told Tucker "I am cramped . . . in the exercise of my own judgment, as to what articles I shall or shall not admit into my work" (J 1:110). On another occasion White objected that Poe had "scarcely selected a passage out of . . . two volumes which warrants the praise he has lavished on it" (J 1:115).[7]

Another difficulty was White's apparently poor financial judgment. This difficulty began with a "household event."

On May 19, according to undisputed records, Virginia Clemm and Edgar Allan Poe were married by the Reverend Amasa Converse, a Presbyterian minister and editor of the *Southern Religious Telegraph*.

Held at the boarding house where Poe and the Clemms lived in Richmond, the ceremony was attended by White and his daughter Eliza. After Virginia and Edgar returned from a brief honeymoon in Petersburg, Mrs. Clemm agreed to rent a house for which White had paid $10,000, and to board the White family and her own. The plan was acceptable to both White, whose wife was an invalid, and to Poe, who had previously paid $9.00 a week for his and the Clemms' board. White decided subsequently that the house was big enough for only one family, and the domestic economy was not effected (J 1:11). On June 7 Poe asked Kennedy for a hundred-dollar loan to pay for furniture he had bought for the scheme (O 1:95). Poe stated that he was in debt "to a small amount, without the means of discharging it upon which I had depended." Six months later, in letters of November 24 and December 15, White himself is complaining that "we are all without money in Richmond," that he is ill, and that there is a printer's strike. White's financial problems may not have extended to all of Richmond in 1836, but by 1837 the nation's economy was in a period of "severe contraction" and Poe had left the *Messenger*. "He retired," White wrote in a January 23 letter to Scott, "on the 3rd instant" (Quinn, pp. 259-60).

In September 1836 the issue of the *Messenger* had been delayed, "owing to the illness of both Publisher and Editor" (Quinn, p. 257). Later, December 27, in a letter to Tucker, White said that Poe had been notified in September that the connection was dissolved.[8] But the break was temporary, since the record shows that in October Poe was back at work. There was, however, no December issue. Poe was drinking again. White's December 27 letter to Tucker was very different from the one White had written to Minor during the Christmas season of the year before:

> Highly as I really think of Poe's talents, I shall be forced to give him notice, in a week or so at farthest, that I can no longer recognize him as editor of my Messenger. Three months ago I felt it my duty to give him a similar notice — and was afterwards overpersuaded to restore him to his situation on certain conditions — which conditions he has again forfeited. [J 1:110]

A letter from Poe four years later substantiates White's letters for the Richmond period. Poe's letter even confirms the announcement of his illness and White's references to his editor's neglect of "certain conditions" — sobriety. The letter, dated April 1, 1841, is to Dr. Joseph Evans Snodgrass, a Baltimore editor who had offered Poe help in legal action he was considering in response to what he called "slanders." The "slanders" were about how much he drank. Poe wrote:

> . . . You are a physician, and I presume no physician can have difficulty in detecting the *drunkard* at a glance. You are, moreover, a literary man, well read in morals. You will never be brought to believe that I could write what I daily write, *as* I write it, were I as this villain would induce those who know me not, to believe. In fine, I pledge you, before God, the solemn word of a gentleman, that I am temperate even to rigor. . . . [O 1:156-57]

Poe then stated that in "candor" he was providing information he believed to be the basis of the slander:

> . . . for a brief period, while I resided in Richmond, and edited the *Messenger*, I certainly did give way, at long intervals, to the temptation held out on all sides by the spirit of Southern conviviality. My sensitive temperament could not stand an excitement which was an everyday matter to my companions. In short, it sometimes happened that I was completely intoxicated. For some days after each excess I was invariably confined to bed. But it is now quite four years since I have abandoned every kind of alcoholic drink — four years, with the exception of a single deviation, which occurred shortly *after* my leaving Burton [whose magazine Poe edited from May 1839 to May 1840], and when I was induced to resort to the occasional use of *cider*, with the hope of relieving a nervous attack.
> You will thus see, frankly stated, the whole amount of my sin. . . .

On the basis of prior evidence for the Richmond period, Poe's statement about excessive intoxication, even though it is excused on the grounds of sociability, is reliable. It is also significant that Poe revealed behavior similar to that during the Richmond experience — when the relationship with an employer became increasingly unsatisfactory, he could not maintain habits of temperance. By his own testimony, then, he was at least "a secondary alcoholic" who "got drunk" in periods of crisis. But he made no connection between job crisis and drinking pattern. (In spite of the characterization of himself as a man of heightened sensibility, he did not recall the earlier melancholy or speak of a recurrence of "the depression of spirits.") Furthermore, Poe interpreted the drinking of cider — to use the language of a twentieth-century physician, William Ober[9] — "as a symptom of an ill-directed therapy rather than the cause" of nervous attacks. It seems reasonable to accept the view that the work he had done, as well as the accuracy of the account of drinking and sickness that followed it, would plead for him. Finally, whatever the tone of the phrase "my sin," Poe was not to use it again in explanations of his drinking. Nor was he to speak of it as a "moral" concern.

Poe had already looked into at least one contemporary medical study on alcoholism. The narrator of *Arthur Gordon Pym* (1838) describes the "state of weakness and horror, brought on by the [port] wine" he and his companions have drunk when they are aboard a destitute ship (H 3:119). To revive and invigorate himself, he plunges into the sea and thereafter immerses the companions. "This idea of sudden immersion," Pym says, "had been suggested to me by reading in some medical work the good effect of the shower-bath in a case where the patient was suffering from *mania a potu* [sic]."

Other of Poe's personae indicate a familiarity with medical texts. The narrator of "Ligeia" (1838) speaks of efforts to restore the dying Rowena by the use of "every exertion which experience, and no little medical reading, could suggest" (H 2:266). In "The Premature Burial" (1844) the narrator has for several years suffered "the singular disorder . . . physicians have agreed to term catalepsy"; although "both the immediate and predisposing causes, and even the actual diagnosis of this disease are still mysterious, its obvious and apparent character is sufficiently well understood." Describing the obvious character, at length, he comments: "My own case differed in no important particular from those mentioned in medical books" (H 5:265). Poe himself, reviewing a book on *Human Magnetism* in 1845, advised: "Those who wish to examine all sides of the question would do well to dip into some medical authority before forming an opinion on such topics" (H 12:123). Poe's interest in other sciences and pseudo-sciences has often been investigated. That interest included one of his central subjects — studies of mania.

Poe was sufficiently critical of failures in the treatment of the insane to satirize a *Maison de santé* ("or private mad-house, about which I had heard much . . . from my medical friends") in "The System of Dr. Tarr and Prof. Fether" (1845). The narrator describes a young woman of whom he says that he cannot be sure she is sane: "She replied in a perfectly rational manner to all that I said, and even her original observations were marked with the soundest good sense; but a long acquaintance with the metaphysics of *mania*, had taught me to put no faith in such evidence of sanity . . ." (H 6:53-55). She was, of course, insane.

Not the least of the variables in the foregoing references to medicine is the term "mania." Since the general sense of the word, according to Ober (p. 204), encompasses "a wide range of attitudes, from folly through controllable impulses to overt psychosis, it is not a restrictive term." Poe's first use of it in the phrase *"mania à potu,"* in *Pym*, is associated with the consequences of drinking port. The ambiguous phrase "metaphysics of *mania*" calls into question judgments of insanity as well as sanity. The narrator's remark and the subject of the satire, however, add to the traces of Poe's evident interest in medical theories and abnormal psychology.

There are, furthermore, other sources that confirm Poe's acquaintance with psychopathology in relation to his perceptions of himself. There is not, so far as is known, a source similar to White's for verification of Poe's account of the history of his problems with alcoholism; there is in his letters, however, the self-acknowledged experience of insanity.

The precise onset of mental illness is a diagnostic problem, and the problem is intensified by the lacunae in the biography of Poe. He continued, it is known, to have at least periodic difficulties connected with drinking in times of stress. In early March 1843, for instance, he went to Washington to meet people influential with President John Tyler who would, Poe hoped, appoint him to a government job. He became intoxicated, then ill, and thereby spoiled the chance for which he and his friends had been making careful arrangements months ahead (O 1:229). Poe's friend Frederick W. Thomas wrote about the fiasco:

> Poor fellow a place had been promised his friends for him, and in that state of suspense . . . he presented himself in Washington certainly not in a way to advance his interests. I have seen a great deal of Poe, and it was his excessive, and at times marked sensibility which forced him into his "frolics," rather than any mere marked appetite for drink, but if he took but one glass of weak wine or beer or cider the Rubicon of the cup was passed with him, and it almost always ended in excess and sickness. [O 1:230]

Captain Mayne Reid, who knew Poe for two years beginning in 1843 in Philadelphia, also wrote tolerantly about Poe's behavior on other occasions:

> I have been his companion on one or two of his wildest frolics, and can certify that they never went beyond the innocent mirth in which we all indulge when Bacchus gets the better of us. With him the jolly-god sometimes played fantastic tricks — to the stealing away his brain, and sometimes, too, his hat — leaving him to walk bareheaded through the streets. . . . While acknowledging this as one of Poe's failings I can speak truly of its not being habitual; only occasional, and drawn out by some accidental circumstances — now disappointment, now the concurrence of a social crowd whose flattering friendship might lead to champagne, a single glass of wine used to affect him so much that he was hardly any longer responsible for his actions, or the disposal of his hat.[10]

Trying and at least partially succeeding in the effort to understand Poe's behavior, these friends do not take into account the full seriousness of Poe's condition. It is from Poe himself that further explanations come.

The biographical events are important. In January 1842 Virginia Poe burst a blood vessel while she was singing, her life was in danger from the bleeding, and Poe himself soon became ill. From February of 1841 he had been one of the editors of *Graham's Magazine* in Philadelphia and had been impressively productive and successful as a writer. When Poe returned to the office after the crisis at home, he found that Charles J. Peterson, another of *Graham's* editors, had taken over. "This so upset Poe that he quit at once, ceasing with the May [1842] number to be a regular editor" (M 551-52). Poe's career, even when marked by a number of dramatic successes, was never again as secure and stable as it was during the period of *Graham's*.[11] Poe never fully recovered from the crisis of 1842. Virginia Poe died five years later on January 30, 1847.

Poe gave a brief account of those years in a letter written on January 4, 1848, to George W. Eveleth. A medical student, Eveleth was a sympathetic young man with whom Poe corresponded about both literary and personal topics. Poe wrote:

> You say — "Can you *hint* to me what was that terrible evil which caused the irregularities so profoundly lamented?" Yes; I can do more than hint. This "evil" was the greatest which could befall a man. Six years ago, a wife, whom I loved as no man ever loved before, ruptured a blood-vessel in singing. Her life was despaired of. I took leave of her forever and underwent all the agonies of her death. She recovered partially and I again hoped. At the end of the year the vessel broke again — I went through precisely the same scene. Again in about a year afterward. Then again— again— again and even once again at varying intervals. Each time I felt the agonies of her death — and at each accession of the disorder I loved her more dearly & clung to her life with more desperate pertinacity. But I am constitutionally sensitive — nervous in a very unusual degree. I became insane, with long periods of horrible sanity. During these fits of absolute unconsciousness I drank, God only knows how often or how much. [O 2:356]

Allowing for histrionic phrasing and exaggerated statements, one recognizes both a genuine and prolonged personal crisis. There is no reason to doubt that Poe was making an effort to explain as honestly as he could what he understood about himself. There is, if nothing else, the true look of agony, even when the appeal is to a person upon whom Poe feels he can rely for understanding also. Poe is no longer speaking in moral terms, he is speaking of insanity to a medical student. The letter continues: "As a matter of course, my enemies referred the insanity to the drink rather than the drink to the insanity."[12] The distinction is not merely defensive or clever wording, but is in fact a good nineteenth-century analysis from authoritative medical studies.

Poe concludes the autobiographical letter as follows:

> I had indeed, nearly abandoned all hope of a permanent cure when I found one in the *death* of my wife. This I can & do endure as becomes a man — it was the horrible never-ending oscillation between hope and despair which I could *not* longer have endured without the total loss of reason. In the death of what was my life, then, I received a new but — oh God! how melancholy existence.

There are also two letters from Poe to Mrs. Clemm in the summer of the next year, 1849, before his death in Baltimore on October 7, 1849. These letters indicate further the extent of Poe's illness and his conception of it. One dated July 7 and written, it is believed, from Philadelphia, begins "My *dear, dear* Mother":

> I have been so ill — have had the cholera, or spasms quite as bad, and can now hardly hold the pen. . . .
>
> It is no use to reason with me *now*; I must die. I have no desire to live since I have done "Eureka." I could accomplish nothing more. For your sake it would be sweet to live, but we must die together. You have been all in all to me, darling, ever beloved mother, and dearest, truest friend.
>
> I was never *really* insane, except on occasions where my heart was touched. . . .
>
> I have been taken to prison once since I came here for getting drunk; but *then* I was not. It was about Virginia. [O 2:452]

The other letter, dated July 19, was written from Richmond:

> My Own Beloved Mother —
>
> You will see at once, by the handwriting of this letter, that I am much better — much better in health and spirits. . . . Most of my suffering arose from that terrible idea which I could not get rid of — the idea that you were dead. For more than ten days I was totally deranged, although I was not drinking one drop; and during this interval I imagined the most horrible calamities. . . .
>
> All was hallucinations, arising from an attack which I had never before experienced — an attack of *mania à potu* [sic]. May Heaven grant that it prove a warning to me for the rest of my days. If so,

> I shall not regret even the horrible unspeakable torments I have endured. . . . [O 2:455]

It had been more than ten years since the casual reference to reading "in some medical work" about the treatment of a "patient suffering from *mania a potu*." It had been almost fourteen years since the critical period of intemperance as well as melancholy and depression such as he had never felt before. Able to recover sufficiently from the crisis in the beginning of his career to continue as a professional writer, he struggled to understand himself, succeeded in recognizing that he drank to excess when he was troubled, and suffered the acknowledged derangement of consciousness which he was unable to survive beyond the age of forty. He had, in fact, both a long and a brief acquaintance with the "metaphysics of mania."

Poe's ironic use of the term "metaphysics" with regard to mania reverberates in relation to his own psychopathology and other considerations as well. Commenting in 1846 on the question "What is poetry?" he wrote that "in the existing condition of metaphysics," the answer "never *can* be settled to the satisfaction of the majority; for the question is purely metaphysical, and the whole science of metaphysics is at present a chaos, through the impossibility of fixing the meaning of the words which its very nature compels it to employ" (H 16:11). (The old definitions, then, were no longer a solace, or a certainty.)

But Poe made whatever use he could of the chaos, that which he experienced and that which he knew from the metaphysicians of disordered cerebration. The July 19 letter to Mrs. Clemm concludes simply:

> B_____ procured me a ticket as far as Baltimore, and the passage from there to Richmond was seven dollars. I have not drank [sic] anything since Friday morning, and then only a little Port wine. *If possible*, dearest Mother, I *will* extricate from this difficulty for your *dear, dear* sake. So keep up heart. . . . When I get my mind a little more composed, I will try to write something. . . .

3

Although references in the fiction to "medical books" and "medical friends" are general, there were at least three specific sources that Poe could have consulted for an understanding of his own history of drinking and illness. The letters revealing that history use both the vocabulary and theories advanced by the three American doctors who gave attention to alcoholism as a mental disease.

Benjamin Rush, the physician, teacher, and reformer who was a signer of the Declaration of Independence, published *Medical Inquiries and Observations upon the Diseases of the Mind* in 1812.[13] This was the first systematic American book on the subject. A pioneer in the rational treatment of mental illness as well as in other aspects of medicine, Rush initiated study of alcoholism even earlier than the publication of the clinical work on diseases of the mind. It was Rush who first took the view that alcoholism was to be attributed to insanity.

As late as 1858 D. Meredith Reese, in "A Report on Moral Insanity in Its Relations to Medical Jurisprudence" published in *Transactions of the American Medical Association*, volume 11, cited Rush as an authority. Reese summarized Rush's contribution as follows:

> That distinguished philosopher and philanthropist, Dr. Benjamin Rush, before the commencement of the present century, seems to have been the first to recognize that form of insanity, since called dipsomania, and, indeed, he preceded Pinel himself, in pleading for habitual drunkards, by ascribing their follies and crimes to moral insanity, which he defined as "derangement of the moral faculty or morbid operations of the will." . . . He declared all such to be monomaniacs, the victims of physical disease, which he, with philosophical accuracy, located in the brain. He taught that, although their drinking habits were the fruit of moral depravity at first, yet after the brain itself had become diseased, by this vice of indulgence, their continued drinking was the result of insanity.[14]

Dr. Charles Caldwell, once a pupil, then a friend, and finally an antagonist of Rush, followed him in the unconventional view of alcoholism. Caldwell, who founded the medical department at Transylvania University, was also a crusader. He is especially known as a polemicist for phrenology, which was taken as "a serious, inductive discipline . . . by many eminent scientists, doctors, and educators" in Poe's time and was considered by at least one distinguished biologist to be "the true science of the mind" as late as 1899.[15] In the second study to be done in the United States on the subject of drinking, "Thoughts on the Pathology, Prevention and Treatment of Intemperance, As a Form of Mental Derangement" (1832), Caldwell referred to the more general and inveterate condition as *"mania à potu."*[16] Caldwell said that "the drunkard was as truly a monomaniac as the one who was sound in other conceptions yet believed his feet and legs were made of glass or butter or his head of copper. Such a person could no more resist the propensity to drink than the other monomaniacs could dissolve the hallucinations that beset them."

Isaac Ray also recognized *mania à potu* in *A Treatise on the Medical*

Jurisprudence of Insanity, first published in 1838. Ray, whose early enthusiastic interest in phrenology abated when he found it of no service in treatment of the mentally ill, was one of the founders of the first national medical organization that became the American Psychiatric Association. The treatise on mental diseases was the outstanding book in the field for over a generation.[17] In it Ray devoted a chapter to medical studies of drunkenness.

After noting the immediate effect of drinking on the mind, Ray discussed "how the long-continued use of alcohol affects the moral and intellectual powers." The account of the pathological effects of drunkenness, he wrote, "would be incomplete without some mention of that curious disease to which it often leads, called *delirium tremens* or *mania à potu.*" Ray then described the illness:

> It may be the immediate effect of an excess or series of excesses in those who are not habitually intemperate, as well as in those who are; but it most commonly occurs in habitual drinkers after a few days of total abstinence from spirituous liquors. It is also very liable to occur in this latter class when laboring under other diseases or severe external injuries that give rise to any degree of constitutional disturbance. The approach of the disease is generally indicated by a slight tremor or faltering of the hands and lower extremities, a tremulousness of the voice, a certain restlessness and sense of anxiety which the patient knows not how to describe or account for, disturbed sleep, and impaired appetite. [Pp. 300-303]

Ray also described the fact that the victim suffered from hallucinations:

> . . . the patient ceases to sleep altogether and soon becomes delirious. . . . The character of the delirium in this disease is peculiar, bearing a stronger resemblance to dreaming than any other form of mental derangement. It would seem as if the dreams which disturb and harass the mind during the imperfect sleep that precede the explosion of the disease continue to occupy it when awake, being then viewed as realities instead of dreams. [P. 301]

Ray argued that "it may be now considered a well-established fact that the habitual drunkard has always more or less of cerebral disease." He states: "Obviously, as these pathological changes are the effect of a long-continued voluntary habit, there is strong evidence in favor of the idea that they, in turn, become efficient causes and act powerfully in maintaining this habit, even in spite of the resistance of the will" (p. 303). He further noted that it "is now well understood that this vice sometimes assumes a periodical character, persons indulging in the greatest excesses periodically who are perfectly sober during the intervals, which may be from the space of a month to that of a year" (p. 304).

Finally Ray discussed the view that there was a category of cases that "originated in pathological causes," but that there was also "another class of cases which strongly point to the same origin and present a close affinity, both in this respect and in that of their symptoms." Poe could well have believed he belonged to the second group: "the persons who are habitually sober" but "are irresistibly impelled to indulge in reckless, unlimited use of intoxicating drinks, whenever agitated by strong emotions" (p. 307).

It can be argued that it sounds as if Isaac Ray had simply anticipated Poe and that Poe was no different from alcoholics any careful observer can describe: Poe was giving an account of himself regardless of the theories of the medical books. But Poe's point that the drink followed the insanity in the explanation of his behavior to Eveleth, the medical student, is shared by Rush, Caldwell, and Ray. When Poe modified the explanation by writing to Maria Clemm that he was never really insane except on occasions where his heart was touched, the remarks coincided with Ray's observation of the cases "agitated by strong emotions."

What has been proved except that Poe became self-analytical? He was, after all, a writer who spoke accurately about himself. Because such terms as "totally deranged" and *"mania à potu"* and even "intervals" which belong to the discussion by Caldwell and Ray were in the air, Poe could have heard them from any medical man conversant with the studies of his time. Poe, however, could also have read the studies in an effort not uncommon among disturbed persons to exhaust available sources for understanding themselves. The use of technical terms in the final letter written to Mrs. Clemm when Poe had been in a state of acute suffering suggests that they are terms to which he was accustomed without question. And although he brought the authority of personal experience to the use of them, he did not make them up. They belonged to his time.

4

Poe's use of the medical concepts of his time to describe his own conditions in letters and his references to medical books in his work suggest that as a writer he also exploited scientific sources in some of the subjects of the horror tales central to the controversies that pervade judgments of him as a literary figure.

In the perspective of twentieth-century enthusiasm for psychological investigations of literature, Poe's stories were fated to be interpreted as both unconscious and conscious expressions of a morbid personal history. A primary example is one of the first of his terrible stories, "Berenice" (1835). Egaeus, the narrator of the tale, "doubtless reproduces in compact and exaggerated form," according to the classic, Freudian analysis by Mme. Marie Bonaparte, "several psycho-neurotic traits of his creator."[18] The story, nonetheless, troubles Mme. Bonaparte, because Egaeus "unites in his person the conflicting symptoms of various mental disorders." In psychoanalytic terminology, Egaeus has "schizoid tendencies" as well as tendencies to "obsessional ruminations" and "an epileptoid attack, followed, as is generally the case, by amnesia." How can so many disorders in one character be explained? "Doubtless," Mme. Bonaparte concludes, "this improbable transformation of an obsessional schizoid into an epileptic, with subsequent amnesia, to some extent symbolizes the infantile amnesia that marked the unconscious sources from which Poe drew this frightful tale" (pp. 213-17). Another twentieth-century critic of the story, Joseph Wood Krutch, believed that in it Poe "understands from the promptings of his own soul that dangerous alchemy, not investigated by scientists until Poe had lain many years in his grave, by which love is transformed into bloody hate."[19]

Poe's story, however, belongs to a nineteenth-century context. The setting, the relationship between Egaeus and Berenice, many of the details, the allusions and tone, are Poesque, but there are also parallels with studies of the pathology and symptoms of mania in Poe's period.

Egaeus and Berenice, as cousins, grew up together in the "gloomy, grey, hereditary halls" of Egaeus's father (H 11:16-26). "Yet differently we grew — I, ill of health, and buried in gloom — she, agile, graceful and overflowing with energy. . . ." Suddenly a fatal disease, followed by a number of maladies including "a species of epilepsy," effected an alteration "in the moral condition of Berenice." "In the meantime," Egaeus recounts, "my own disease — for I have been told that I should call it by no other appellation — my own disease, then, grew rapidly upon me, and assumed finally a monomaniac character of a novel and extraordinary form — hourly and momently gaining vigor — and at length obtaining over me the most incomprehensible ascendency."

The focus of the story, then, is on what Egaeus describes as "the disordered chamber of my brain" and "my case." "This monomania, if I must so term it," Egaeus notes, "consisted in a morbid irritability of those properties of the mind in metaphysical science termed the *attentive*." He thinks it more than probable he is not understood, but fears that it is not possible to convey to the general reader "an adequate idea of that nervous *intensity of interest* with which . . . the powers of meditation (not to speak technically) busied and buried themselves, in the contemplation of even the most ordinary objects of the universe." He could, for instance, muse for hours on a frivolous device in the margin of a book or dream away whole days over the perfume of a flower and "lose all sense of motion or physical existence by means of absolute bodily quiescence. . . ." Such vagaries exercising the "attentive" as distinguished from the "speculative" faculty of the mind, Egaeus notes, were "not, indeed, altogether unparalleled," but defied analysis or explanation.

These experiences were followed, according to Egaeus, by "the full fury of my monomania," against "the strange and irresistible influence" of which he struggled in vain. Of all the objects of the universe, he came to have no thought for any but Berenice's teeth: "For these I longed with a frenzied desire." With little or almost no awareness of what happened thereafter, Egaeus remembers only that Berenice had succumbed to an epileptic trance, was thought dead, and prepared for burial. He later learns that he had violated the grave, mutilated her in order to extract her teeth, and killed her. The "impress of human nails" on one of Egaeus's hands leaves no doubt of the horror of the struggle.

Whatever reasons Poe had for telling the story, he indicates through Egaeus himself at least a simple medical knowledge of the subject. When the narrator says he will not speak technically, he uses the knowledge without relying totally on metaphysical science. Isaac Ray, in the extensive review of the studies of insanity in Poe's period, noted that the term "monomania" to refer to "partial intellectual mania" was in general use in medical literature by 1838, although the term had recently replaced "melancholia" by which "the ancients" called the disease.[20] Poe also uses the doctrine of "irritation" advocated by François J. V. Broussais (1772-1830), professor of medicine at the University of Paris (Ray, pp. 106, 148). When Egaeus says that the monomania "consisted in a morbid irritability" and recalls an absolute bodily quiescence followed by "the frenzied desire" for Berenice's teeth, he is exemplifying the theory that "irritation . . . is the initial stage of disease — the first in a chain of events of which disorganization is the last. . . ." Furthermore, the "departure from the normal course of vital action, which is probably as unexceptional a definition of irritation as can be given, is sufficient to derange the part in which it occurs. . . ."

The fact that the disease had its incomprehensible aspects did not contradict the most advanced medical opinion of the early nineteenth century. "To determine exactly what mental impairment it is which is essential to insanity, metaphysicians and physiologists have long and anxiously labored with hardly the shadow of success" (Ray, p. 120).

Little was known beyond the single fact, according to Ray, that "mania arises from a morbid affection of the brain," or "a disease of the brain" (p. 104). Poe's method — to have Egaeus describe the course of the disease and its consequences for him — does not differ in essence from the medical studies of the time. The principal writers on insanity, of whom Ray lists eighteen, including French, English, German, Danish, and American physicians, described the various phenomena of mania, referred them (often with the qualification "as far as our knowledge will permit") to particular faculties, and illustrated them with cases.

If Poe's narrator seems to unite "the conflicting symptoms" of several mental disorders, one possible explanation can be found in a review of the studies of the period. When the physicians themselves write about kinds of mania, terms vary, bases of classification are shifted, views are retracted or modified, meanings overlap or are vague, and some cases do not fit categories. Ray, for instance, follows J. E. D. Esquirol's distinction between two kinds of homicidal insanity, or "monomania-homicide," in one of which "the monomaniac is always influenced by avowed motives more or less irrational and is generally regarded as mad"; in the other "there are no motives acknowledged nor to be discerned, the individual being impelled by a blind, irresistible impulse" (p. 148). Ray argues, however, that "this division has not been strictly made by nature, cases often occurring that do not clearly come under either category," so the subject will be "better elucidated" by noticing all the forms of the disease, which he then illustrates by cases. Poe's Egaeus belongs, in part, to both categories. The motive for the murder is the irrational desire for the teeth: "Ah," he says, "here was the idiotic thought that destroyed me. . . . I coveted them madly! I felt that their possession could alone ever restore me to peace, in giving me back to reason." Avowing the motive, he cannot — without being inconsistent in his rational account — consider himself impelled "by a blind, irresistible impulse," but he did speak of the "strange and irresistible influence" against which he struggled.

Another likely reason for the fact that Egaeus seems, to a later student of mental illness, an improbable case is that Poe apparently hashed together material from more than one source. Benjamin Rush, the principal American writer before Ray on "mental medicine," makes a number of observations that Poe could easily have known. Rush, for instance, discusses "partial insanity, or false perception on one subject, while the judgment is sound and correct upon all others."[21] Although Rush's terms are not used by Poe, he has taken care to create a narrator who gives an ironically rational account of what he understands about the history of the disease; the coherence of the account tends to leave one with the conviction that Egaeus is a reliable witness, whether he is or not. Rush

ith respect to persons suffering from partial insanity, that as
t their judgment is not affected by this defect they will both
and lament their crime when detected. In the course of recounting
session with "*the teeth* of the changed Berenice" Egaeus exclaims:
d to God that I had never beheld them, or that, having done so, I
d!"[22]

h also provides a prosaic basis for both the most esoteric and the
melodramatic aspects of Poe's story. Outlining various characteristics of "moral derangement" in relation to kinds of murders committed
by the deranged, Rush makes at least three points particularly pertinent
to details in "Berenice." Rush states that the murder "is usually committed upon near relations, and friends; and often by persons of the most
exemplary moral and religious characters"; that it "is sometimes committed by persons under the influence of delusive opinions in religion"; and
the "circumstances of greater and more deliberate cruelty attend it, than
common murders."[23]

Perhaps the theory of Rush as well as the fact that Poe later was to
marry his cousin Virginia was responsible for the fiction in which Egaeus
and Berenice were not only to be married but were also cousins. Egaeus
says of the relationship that during "the brightest days of her unparalleled
beauty, most surely I had never loved her. . . . Yet, bitterly lamenting
her fallen and desolate condition, I called to mind that she had loved me
long, and, in an evil moment, I spoke to her of marriage." An animist who
believed in the previous existence of souls, Egaeus comes from a race of
visionaries, is addicted "to the most intense and painful meditation," and
has spent his life in "the wild dominions of monastic thought and erudi-
tion." Of the books he was reading at the time that the mania was developing, he states: "If they did not actually serve to irritate the disorder,
[they] partook, it will be perceived, largely, in their imaginative and in-
consequential nature, of the characteristic qualities of the disorder itself."
He well remembers that he read: "the treatise of the noble Italian, Coelius
Secundus Curio, '*De Amplitudine Beati Regni Dei*'; St Austin's great
work, 'The City of God'; and Tertullian's '*De Carne Christi.*' " Such details, the elaborations of Poe, seem less esoteric and more understandable
in the context of the analyses of Rush. Poe makes a subtle connection
between the "religious" interests of Egaeus and the murder he commits.
Poe does not imply that Egaeus murders Bernice because he was under the
influence of delusive opinions in religion, but suggests by the interest
that Egaeus was a person of exemplary moral and religious character. And
because Egaeus was a visionary, an "inversion" took place in the character
of his commonest thought: the realities of the world affected him "as
visions, . . . while the wild ideas of the land of dreams, became, in turn,

not the material of . . . every-day existence, but . . . that existence utterly and solely in itself." The reading which he did occupied him in the escape from reason and contributed to its being "shaken from its balance." The parallel between the cruelty of the act Egaeus perpetrates and the comments by Rush gives an extra-autobiographical authority to the shocking conclusion of the mania Poe has depicted.

If Poe's experience of melancholy in the fall of 1835 is thought to inform the description of Egaeus as a man "ill of health and buried in gloom," it should be remembered that "Berenice" was published in March of that year. If it is thought that Poe projects an oncoming depression or fear of it in the story, his lack of insight with regard to the early symptoms of his mental disturbances is telling, and does not argue strongly for a self-conscious expression of presentiments. No matter what unconscious forces moved Poe to choose the subject of the story, or to develop the crudely sensational consequences of the situation in what he calls its "novel and extraordinary form," he must have pilfered as he pleased, and freely but scrupulously modified medical studies with which the story has so much in common. In view of the fact that the story fulfills all the conditions in Rush's analysis — the partial insanity which is acknowledged, the murder of a near relation, the circumstances including the visionary character of Egaeus and the cruelty of the act which he laments — the fiction is convincing evidence that Poe was consciously dependent on medical theory.

"Berenice," moreover, is particularly significant in Poe's career as a writer because the story launched him in the kind of subject he was later to treat with unquestionable coherence, understanding, lucidity, and skill. The story, for example, prefigures "The Fall of the House of Usher" (1839). Even though Cleanth Brooks and Robert Penn Warren criticize the story of Usher on the grounds that he is "a clinical case" (about which they are right) and object that "The Fall" exemplifies horror for its own sake[24] (a judgment which Poe himself anticipates), there are other critics who consider the work a fine instance of psychological insight, or "le réalisme des romantiques."[25] In "Berenice," too, Poe not only gives away more obviously than he was to do later the fact that he is drawing on medical studies for at least some of the authority and knowledge of the horror, but also reveals how he worked from sources he found of interest for psychological fiction that justly insured him an important place in American literature.

In "The Fall of the House of Usher," Poe's narrator received a "wildly importunate" letter from Usher who "spoke of acute bodily illness — of a mental disorder which oppressed him — and of an earnest desire to see me . . . with a view of attempting, by the cheerfulness of my society, some alleviation of his malady" (H 3:273-97). The narrator, who responds to Usher's invitation, describes supposedly without benefit of medical study another case of monomania. The term itself is not used in the story. The narrator refers instead to "the melancholy of my friend," his "highly distempered identity" and "disordered fancy," "the kingdom of disorganization," or "an observable change" that "came over the features of the mental disorder of my friend." The observer also calls Usher a "hypochondriac" and says that "there was a species of mad hilarity in his eyes — an evidently restrained *hysteria* in his whole demeanor." Like Egaeus, Usher would sit dreaming for hours over books. Usher's "chief delight . . . was found in the perusal of an exceedingly rare and curious book in quarto Gothic — the manual of a forgotten church — the *Vigiliae Mortuorum secundum Chorum Ecclesiae Maguntinae* ['The Watches of the Dead, according to the Choir of the Church of Mayence'] ." Echoing a comment of Egaeus about the relation between the reading and the mania, the narrator says, "I could not help thinking of the wild ritual of this work, and of its probable influence upon the hypochondriac. . . ." Like Egaeus, too, Usher believes in animism: "I lack words," the narrator notes, "to express the full extent, or the earnest *abandon* of his persuasion."

Varying some of the salient details from the account of Egaeus, Poe also develops a number of significant differences in Usher's story. A major difference is effected through the narrator-observer. He allows Poe to adhere to a physician's principle of diagnosis with respect to mania.

An individual whose sanity is in question, Isaac Ray advises, is "to be compared with himself" (pp. 110-12). Ray writes: "Madness is not indicated so much by a particular extravagance of thought or feeling, as by a well-marked change of character or departure from the ordinary habits of thinking, feeling, acting. . . ." Abstract mental states, he points out, are not in themselves proofs of lunacy. "It is," Ray warns, "not the abstract act or feeling which constitutes a *symptom;* it is the departure from the natural and healthy character, temper and habits, that gives it this meaning. . . . Mania . . . is generally preceded . . . by a change in the natural conditions. . . ."

"Surely," Poe's narrator comments, "man had never before so terribly altered, in so brief a period, as had Roderick Usher! It was with difficulty that I could bring myself to admit the identity of the wan being before me with the companion of my early boyhood." The narrator then describes the relation of Usher's present state to what Ray would call his "natural, habitual state" (p. 110). "In the manner of my friend," the narrator observes, "I was at once struck with an incoherence — an inconsistency; and I soon found this to arise from a series of feeble and futile struggles to overcome an habitual trepidancy — an excessive nervous agitation. For something of this nature I had indeed been prepared . . . by reminiscences of certain boyish traits, and by conclusions deduced from his peculiar physical conformation and temperament." For the comparison of Usher with the boy remembered, the narrator gives a full description:

> . . . The character of his face had been at all times remarkable. A cadaverousness of complexion; an eye large, liquid, and luminous beyond comparison; lips somewhat thin and very pallid, but of surpassingly beautiful curve; a nose of delicate Hebrew model, but with a breadth of nostril unusual in similar formations; a finely moulded chin, speaking, in its want of prominence, of a want of moral energy; hair of a more than web-like softness and tenuity; — these features, with an inordinate expansion above the regions of the temple, made up altogether a countenance not easily to be forgotten.

The change in Usher has been well prepared.

> And now in the mere exaggeration of the prevailing character of these features, and of the expression they were wont to convey, lay so much of change that I doubted to whom I spoke. The now ghastly pallor of the skin, and the now miraculous lustre of the eye, above all things startled and even awed me. The silken hair, too, had been suffered to grow all unheeded, and as, in its wild gossamer texture, it floated rather than fell about the face, I could not, even with effort, connect its Arabesque expression with any idea of simple humanity.

Adhering to good medical practice in the response to the visually shocking Usher, Poe leaves no doubt that "the abstract mental state" of Usher is one of fear culminating in terror to which not only the change in Usher but the catalepsy of Usher's sister and the desolation of the house contribute. The narrator also experiences the terror, although it is hardly certain that he suffers an aberration of mind or heart. In fact, he recounts that Usher calls him "madman" because of the narrator's failure to discern the reason for the horrendous noises they hear.

While Ray's statements on the principle of diagnosis of mania are to be found in other studies of mental medicine, Ray's discussion of diagnosis concludes with a useful summary of numerous symptoms of physical derangement (p. 114), and affords the most convincing evidence that his work was familiar to Poe. Ray warned that no one patient will "marshall forth every symptom that has at any time been observed in the countless disorders"; by comparison with Ray's analysis, Poe is generous but selective in the striking signs of mania which he uses to verify Usher's abnormal history. In the review of likely symptoms, Ray notes that:

A febrile excitement pervades the system. . . . the eye has a wild and glassy look, the sensations have become either more acute or more obscure. . . . The muscular power is sometimes inordinately developed, the waking moments being a scene of almost constant restlessness and agitation; while at others there is an equally unnatural sluggishness and indisposition to move about. Hunger and thirst are seldom unaffected, the patient either taking immense quantities of food or scarcely sufficient to supply the wants of nature. . . .

Although Poe does not quite follow Ray's order, he is close enough to it to suggest that he had the medical text open on the writing desk while the story of Usher was in process. Usher's "excessive nervous agitation" and "miraculous lustre of the eye" have already been remarked. Usher tells the narrator that the disease "displayed itself in a host of unnatural sensations." Usher, Poe's narrator elaborates,

suffered much from a morbid acuteness of the senses; the most insipid food was alone endurable; he could wear only garments of certain texture; the odors of all flowers were oppressive; his eyes were tortured by even a faint light; and there were but peculiar sounds . . . which did not inspire him with horror. . . .
. . . .
. . . a morbid condition of the auditory nerve . . . rendered all music intolerable to the sufferer, with the exception of certain effects of stringed instruments.

The narrator also says that Usher's action is "alternately vivacious and sullen." The description of Usher's voice continues as an illustration of this point and adds another parallel to an earlier passage in Ray. Usher's voice "varied rapidly from a tremulous indecision (when the animal spirits seemed utterly in abeyance) to that species of energetic concision − that abrupt, weighty, unhurried, and hollow-sounding enunciation − that leaden, self-balanced, and perfectly modulated guttural utterance, which may be observed in the lost drunkard, or the irreclaimable eater of opium, during the periods of his most intense excitement." Ray, before listing symptoms of mania, cites E. J. Georget's analysis of the period of incubation which precedes the outbreak of the disease (p. 112). Georget observes that in one category of cases, the patient "as many people do in the first stages of intoxication . . . makes every effort to appear reasonable."

In accordance with Ray's list of symptoms, Poe's narrator also speaks of the fact that Usher

roamed from chamber to chamber with hurried, unequal, and ob-

> jectless step. . . . There were times, indeed, when I thought his un-
> ceasingly agitated mind was laboring with some oppressive secret,
> to divulge which he struggled for the necessary courage. At times,
> again, I was obliged to resolve all into the mere inexplicable vagaries
> of madness, for I beheld him gazing upon vacancy for long hours . . .
> as if listening to some imaginary sound.

Even the allusion to Hamlet's gazing upon vacancy awhile could have been suggested by Ray who observed that Shakespeare's Hamlet is one of the few admirable exceptions to the representation of mania by poets and novelists (p. 244). But the allusion is followed by "as if listening to some imaginary sound." Poe skillfully implies in the delineation of symptoms — in Ray's language "the sensations have become either more acute or more obscure" — that Usher hears his sister, the Lady Madeline, and is laboring with the knowledge, not just the possibility, that when she was interred she was not dead but alive. Poe has outdistanced all medical study, and there is the crux of Poe's method.

The account of Usher's mania is, nevertheless, indebted to medical theory on at least two other points. Ray quotes Georget with respect to the type of patient whose thought only becomes affected gradually and who is "generally conscious of some disorder in his intellectual faculties" (p. 112). Such a patient "feels himself changing in his affections; but, at the same time, he preserves a consciousness of his condition, is vexed at it, and tries to conceal it. . . ." "Sooner or later," Ray notes, "the disorder of the cerebral functions becomes of a more obvious and positive character" (p. 114). Then "the struggle between the convictions of his sounder reason and the impulses of this new condition ceases, and the patient, instead of contending any longer against the approaches of the disease or [instead] of concealing his thoughts, now believes in their reality and openly and strenuously avows them, except when induced by powerful reasons to pursue a contrary course." Upon the narrator's arrival, Usher "entered, at some length, into what he conceived to be the nature of his malady. It was, he said, a constitutional and family evil and one for which he despaired to find a remedy — a mere nervous affection, he immediately added, which would undoubtedly soon pass off." The narrator found Usher a slave to "an anomalous species of terror." Usher states that in "this unnerved, this pitiable condition I feel that the period will sooner or later arrive when I must abandon life and reason together, in some struggle with the grim phantasm, FEAR." In Usher's "rhymed verbal improvisations" — the verses of "The Haunted Palace" — the narrator "fancied" that he perceived "a full consciousness on the part of Usher of the tottering of his lofty reason upon her throne."

Ray provides an additional reason for Poe's narrator. "In common with other diseases," Ray observes, mania may evince "the remedial powers of proper air and exercise, of cheerful conversation, of friendly sympathy and attention, and of employments which furnish a healthful play to the actions of the whole system, and abstract the patient from the contemplation of his own condition" (p. 109). The narrator, it will be remembered, responded to Usher's request for a visit "with a view of attempting, by the cheerfulness of my society, some alleviation" of his illness. In another reference to Ray's theory of treatment, Poe gives away parenthetically a knowledge of the theory. During Usher's crisis before the moment of Madeline's return from her tomb, the narrator reads to Usher. "I indulged a vague hope," the narrator states, "that the excitement which now agitated the hypochondriac, might find relief (for the history of mental disorder is full of similar anomalies). . . ."

Poe's narrator had already despaired of the efficacy of remedial measures. For several days following the premature burial of Usher's sister, the narrator recounted, "I was busied in earnest endeavors to alleviate the melancholy of my friend. We painted and read together, or I listened, as if in a dream, to the wild improvisations of his speaking guitar." Art, to which Poe himself must often have looked for aid, was put to an early test. The narrator's experience, one can guess, carries the authority of Poe's insight or of his anguish in the study of medical texts. The narrator writes of the uses and limitations of the artistic experiences he and Usher shared.

> And thus, as a closer and still closer intimacy admitted me more unreservedly into the recesses of his [Usher's] spirit, the more bitterly did I perceive the futility of all attempt at cheering a mind from which darkness, as if an inherent positive quality, poured forth upon all the objects of the moral and physical universe, in one unceasing radiation of gloom.

Whether or not one accepts the point that "Poe's own fear of mental decay, which came upon him at times, due to his family history, is probably reflected" in "The Fall of the House of Usher,"[26] one must recall that Poe had once suffered from melancholy and at least secondary alcoholism as long as four years before the publication of the story; he had not yet experienced the insanity following Virginia's illness. It is, therefore, reasonable to doubt that he would have had the authority to write as knowledgeably as he does of Usher's illness without solid reliance on the medical specialists of the period. Agreements between Ray's work published in 1838 and Poe's story which came out a year later place the writer among the collaborators in the development of both informed and imaginative understanding of mental illness. To call Poe a collaborator is not to disparage what he contributed in the fiction. He not only grasped the import of the subject, but mastered it responsibly, when it is measured by the best authorities of the period, and, in retrospect, without denial of the risks entailed. The narrator himself speaks for Poe as one of the biographers of the soul: "I," the narrator says simply, "had been passing alone, on horseback, through a singularly dreary tract of country, and at length found myself . . . within the view of the melancholy House of Usher." Furthermore, as if to counter the judgment that the story is horrible for the pleasure of horror, the narrator remarks:

> I know not how it was — but, with the first glimpse of the building, a sense of insufferable gloom pervaded my spirit. I say insufferable; for the feeling was unrelieved by any of that half-pleasurable, because poetic, sentiment, with which the mind usually receives even the sternest natural images of the desolate or terrible. . . . There was an iciness, a sinking, a sickening of the heart — an unredeemed dreariness of thought which no goading of the imagination could torture into aught of the sublime.

Insufferable gloom, desolation, an unredeemed and goaded imagination — these are among Poe's gifts to American literature. "If in many of my productions terror has been the thesis," Poe wrote for the preface to *Tales of the Grotesque and Arabesque* (1840), "I maintain that terror is not of Germany, but of the soul, — that I have induced this terror only from its legitimate sources, and urged it only to its legitimate results." He said, moreover, that he could not "conscientiously claim indulgence on the score of hasty effort." In conclusion, he noted, "I think it best becomes me to say, therefore, that if I have sinned, I have deliberately sinned. These brief compositions [which included "Berenice" and "The Fall of the House of Usher"] are, in chief part, the results of matured purpose and very careful elaboration."

5

Poe's extensive reliance on medical theory for "Berenice" was apparently a kind of trial and apprenticeship, whereas "The Fall of the House of Usher" was proof of a critical command of knowledge that prepared the writer for further development in which he went even less by the books. He continued to rely upon them for concepts, situations, and suggestions, but he was not as apt to use the terminology or to refer even parenthetically to extra-authorial supports. Furthermore, in contrast to the simple tendency to proliferate details seen, for example, in the sketching of Usher's appearance or his "morbid acuteness of the senses," Poe concentrates more attention on the points he selected and allows a detail to grow into a fully realized episode or an entire story. Two notable examples are "The Man of the Crowd" and "The Tell-Tale Heart."

"The Man of the Crowd" (1840) is for Poe's narrator-observer "the type and genius of deep crime. He refuses to be alone" (H 4:134-35). Wandering moodily to and fro, day and night, through the streets of London, the man does not even notice the narrator (who follows to the point of exhaustion) but continues the "solemn walk." He "spoke no word," "seemed lost in thought," was "without apparent aim," and there "was something more intense than despair" to be "observed upon the countenance of the singular being."

Poe's idea for the sketch may have in part derived from Ray's discussion of the case of Papavoine who murdered two young children near Paris in 1823 (pp. 192-94). In Papavoine's trial, "the counsel of the prisoner . . . had pleaded homicidal insanity in his defence," with which Ray agrees. The American physician, quoting from a French study of both the medical and legal aspects of the question, criticizes the advocate-general who "declared that Papavoine committed the crime in order 'to gratify an inveterate hatred against his fellowmen, transformed at first, into a weariness of his own life, and subsequently into an instinct of ferocity and a thirst of blood.' " Ray then argues that the "advocate-general himself represented Papavoine 'as having been noted for his unsocial disposition, for avoiding fellow-laborers, for walking in retired, solitary places, appearing to be much absorbed in the vapors of a black melancholy.' " Ray, however, insists that the advocate-general's characterization "is not a picture of those human fiends" to whom the advocate "would assimilate Papavoine."

As if picking up Ray's disagreement with the lawyer, Poe's narrator says of the countenance and expression of "The Man of the Crowd": "I well remember that my first thought, upon beholding it, was that Retszch [an illustrator of Goethe's *Faust*] . . . would have greatly preferred it to his own pictural incarnations of the fiend." Poe's narrator thinks that the man provokes among other ideas those "of coolness, of malice, of bloodthirstiness, of triumph"; following him because of a desire to know more of the man, the narrator at last feels that the interest is in vain: "I shall learn no more of him, nor of his deeds." Poe's observer never says that the man is mad. Poe, rather, dramatizes in insistent and nearly hypnotic rhythms the main subject of the story — the enigmatic restlessness of an unidentified, wayward, and lonely man. Ray pleads unequivocally for Papavoine; Poe's ambivalent imagination brings "the mad energy" of the man painfully to life.

"The Tell-Tale Heart" (January 1843) is considered one of Poe's most effective stories of terror and helplessness. The narrator of the story has killed an old man (H 5:88-94). The murderer pleads ironically:

> True! — nervous — very, very dreadfully nervous I had been and am! but why *will* you say that I am mad? The disease had sharpened my senses — not destroyed — not dulled them. Above all was the sense of hearing acute. I heard all things in heaven and in earth. I heard many things in hell. How, then, am I mad? Harken! and observe how healthily — how calmly I can tell you the whole story. . . . Now this is the point. You fancy me mad. Madmen know nothing. But you should have seen *me*. You should have seen how wisely I proceeded — with what caution — with what foresight — with what dissimulation I went to work!

There are obvious similarities between Ray's discussions of "moral mania" and the concepts Poe uses here. Ray says of homicidal monomaniacs that although some "plead insanity in defence of their conduct or an entire ignorance of what they did," others "deny that they labored under any such condition, and at most acknowledge only a perturbation of mind" (p. 170). Poe modifies and makes further use of the symptom of "acuteness" of the senses described in Usher, and included in Ray's list as one manifestation of the mania. And it is Ray who reports "a class of cases" that feel "as if bound by a sense of necessity to destroy life; and proceed to the fulfillment of their destiny with the utmost calmness and deliberation" (p. 158).

"It is impossible to say how the idea first entered my brain," Poe's narrator tries to explain after the murder, "but once conceived, it haunted me day and night. Object there was none. Passion there was none. I loved the old man. He had never wronged me. For his gold I had no desire." This analysis recalls the studies of Rush, who outlined the kind of murder committed by a person suffering from "moral derangement, . . . that state of mind in which the passions act involuntarily through the instrumentality of the will. . . ."[27] Such a murder, according to Rush, is committed without a motive: "without provocation, or malice, either of a sudden, or a chronic nature. It is usually committed upon near relations, and friends. . . . It is never accompanied by robbery."

It may be objected that Poe's narrator provides a motive when he tries to account for the murder: "I think it was his eye! Yes, it was this. One of his eyes resembled that of a vulture — a pale blue eye, with a film over it. Whenever it fell upon me, my blood ran cold; and so by degrees — very gradually — I made up my mind to take the life of the old man, and thus rid myself of the eye forever." Ray, following Rush's theory, clarifies the point: "In homicidal insanity murder is committed without any motive whatever deserving the name, or at most, with one totally inadequate to produce the act in a sane mind" (p. 170). Poe is responsible for the obsession with the eye.

Although never kinder to the old man than during the whole week before he killed him, the murderer tortures the victim every night by stealthily opening the door in darkness and then shooting the ray of a lantern into the "evil" eye where he relentlessly holds it for some minutes. Finally, on the eighth night, "the old man's hour had come." The narrator recalls that

> With a loud yell, I threw open the lantern and leaped into the room. He shrieked once – once only. In an instant I dragged him onto the floor, and pulled the heavy bed over him. I then smiled gaily, to find the deed so done. But, for many minutes, the heart beat on with a muffled sound. This, however, did not vex me: . . . at length it ceased. The old man was dead.

The point is again similar to Rush's observation on murder by the morally deranged: "Circumstances of greater and more deliberate cruelty attend it, than common murders."

Poe's murderers never flee. After the old man is safely buried under the floor of the house, officers of the police arrive – a neighbor had been disturbed by the old man's shriek. The police complete their investigation and find nothing; then the narrator, talking with them, hears the heart beat again. No wonder that he bursts out: "'Villains! . . . I admit the deed! – tear up the planks! – here, here!'" Rush's final characterization of the homicidal maniac is that the murder "is never, or rarely, succeeded by an attempt to escape; but, on the contrary, the persons who perpetrate it, generally confess what they have done. . . ." The confessional narrative is the form most frequently used in Poe's fiction; in "The Tell-Tale Heart" the agonist's point of view is developed with an economy and verisimilitude that are as subtle as they are blatant. "The hysterical energy of the opening sentences," D. E. S. Maxwell observes, "is authentically colloquial, modulating to the speaking tones of insanity, which impinges on the outer world in the experience – commonplace enough – of 'a shriek . . . heard by a neighbor during the night' and the police . . . who 'chatted of familiar things.' "[28]

Poe's special contribution to the story includes his exposition of a point one finds Ray mentioning almost as if it were an aside about the cases of moral mania in which "the murderous propensity coexists with hallucination" (p. 170). Recalling the events immediately preceding the murder, the persona insists:

> And now — have I not told you that what you mistake for madness is but over acuteness of the senses? — now, I say, there came to my ears a low, dull, quick sound, such as a watch makes when enveloped in cotton. I knew *that* sound well, too. It was the beating of the old man's heart. It increased my fury, as the beating of a drum stimulates the soldier into courage.
>
> But even yet I refrained and kept still. I scarcely breathed. I held the lantern motionless. I tried how steadily I could maintain the ray upon the eye. Meantime the hellish tattoo of the heart increased. It grew quicker, and louder and louder every instant. The old man's terror *must* have been extreme! It grew louder, I say, louder every moment! — do you mark me well? I have told you that I am nervous: so I am. And now at the dead hour of night, amid the dreadful silence of that old house, so strange a noise as this excited me to uncontrollable terror. Yet, for some minutes longer I refrained and stood still. But the beating grew louder, louder! I thought the heart must burst.

The murder committed, the police having searched the house without discovering the body of the victim, and the murderer confident that he has outwitted the officers, he "desires" them to sit down; as they chat, he is "singularly at ease." But before long, he recounts: "My head ached, and I fancied a ringing in my ears. . . . The ringing became more distinct: — it continued and became more distinct: I talked more freely to get rid of the feeling: but it continued and gained definiteness — until, at length, I found that the noise was *not* within my ears." The narrator gasps for breath; the sound is the old man's heart. In a frenzy of terror the narrator cannot believe the police do not hear the unrelenting beat grow "louder — louder — *louder!*" Possessed by what he hears, he screams out that he is the killer. Ray himself draws on the sixteenth of the *Introductory Lectures* by Dr. Rush, who, when asked to examine a criminal suspected of feigning madness, decided chiefly on finding the prisoner's "pulse twenty beats more frequent than in the natural state" that the man was in fact mad (p. 251). Ray's list of symptoms of mania includes acceleration of the pulse, but Ray also notes that "the patient complains of pain in the head, . . . [and] ringing in the ears" (p. 114).

The differences between medical history and the tortured coherence that reveals a mind at bay suggest a measure of Poe's achievement. "It is Poe's genius," in the judgment of Alan A. and Sue Smart Stone, "that he leaves the reader unsure whether one is witness to the uncanny, or to a psychotic distortion. This is of little consequence since it is this very quality of the uncanny which is so often felt by the psychotic."[29] "The Tell-Tale Heart" was chosen by the Stones to be included in studies of *The Abnormal Personality through Literature* because the story "gives one an insight into the agonizing nature of some hallucinations." It has, in the opinion of Mme. Bonaparte, "sovereign power" (p. 500).

6

The lucidity and insight of "The Tell-Tale Heart" as well as the atmosphere of morbid dread in "The Fall of the House of Usher" do not necessarily imply that the stories are informed by the psychic dissonance of the author. Analyzing similarities between medical texts and Poe's imaginative fusion of concepts which the physicians advanced, one can say at least that the tales do not depend absolutely on biographical fact for their authenticity. One can say, further, that the evidence in his letters — evidence which it seems reasonable to accept — makes it doubtful that the tales published before 1842, "Berenice," "Usher," and "The Man of the Crowd," depend on Poe's actual experience of insanity. Because the time at which his mental illness began after January of 1842 is uncertain, it is not possible to say precisely when the writer could have used that acknowledged experience as a basis for insight into the situations he depicts in the stories published after "The Man of the Crowd." The exact date of composition of " The Tell-Tale Heart" is also uncertain; it was published in January of 1843. Like the earlier work, it could depend largely on Poe's skill in transforming medical theory into fiction.

But Poe, writing in 1848 of the household events that began with Virginia's illness in January of 1842 and its recurrence the next year, said he "became insane, with long periods of sanity," and that during "these fits of absolute unconsciousness" he drank "God only knows how often or how much." On the basis of the account of his secondary alcoholism previously, it is likely that Poe's illness following Virginia's first crisis was related to his drinking. It seems unlikely, however, that the "insanity" developed earlier than Virginia's second illness in 1843, although it is not possible to say with certainty from the evidence available. "The Black Cat" (August 1843) was written in 1842 (H 5:143-55). Since it is the story of a man's "radical alteration" in general temperament and character "through the instrumentality of the Fiend Intemperance," it must be related to, if not prompted by Poe's biography in juxtaposition with his interest in the pathology of alcoholism. Even the most cautious of investigations can legitimately assume that there are conscious connections among medical authority, the narrative, and the voice of experience in "The Black Cat."

The man in the story tells of mutilating, then murdering, a once loyal cat and of finally murdering the uncomplaining, patient, and suffering wife he loved. "From infancy," the narrator recalls, he "was noted for the docility and humanity of his disposition." His "tender-heartedness," in fact, made him "the jest" of his companions. He "was especially fond of animals." He "married early, and was happy to find a wife whose disposition was not uncongenial with" his own and who shared the affection for animals: "birds, goldfish, a fine dog, rabbits, a small monkey," and Pluto, a beautiful, sagacious black cat. The cat was the man's "favorite pet."

As the disease of alcoholism grew upon him during several years, the man became "day by day, more moody, more irritable, more regardless of the feelings of others." "I suffered myself," he says, "to use intemperate language to my wife. At length, I even offered her personal violence. My pets, of course, were made to feel the change in my disposition . . . and at length even Pluto . . . began to experience the effects of my ill-temper."

Returning home from his haunts about town one night, the man was "much intoxicated." He fancied, he relates, that the cat avoided him: "I seized him; when in fright at my violence, he inflicted a slight wound upon my hand with his teeth. . . ." The fury of a demon instantly possessed the man. He knew himself no longer; his "original soul" took flight from his body, and "a more than fiendish malevolence" thrilled every fiber of his frame. He took from his waistcoat pocket a penknife, opened it, grasped the cat by the throat, and deliberately cut one of its eyes from the socket.

First describing the immediate effect of drunkenness on the mind, Isaac Ray includes among the symptoms the point that the intoxicated person "is apt to imagine either that he has offended someone . . . or, that he has been offended, and fixes upon some one as the object of his maledictions, perhaps his blows" (pp. 299-300). Ray then reports on the effects of long-continued use of alcoholic liquors: "Except in some happily organized natures, the original delicacy and acuteness of the moral perceptions are invariably blunted; the relations of neighbor, citizen, father, spouse, have lost their accustomed place in his thoughts; . . . and the finer emotions of the soul, which will occasionally be felt by the least cultivated minds, have entirely deserted his nature." Poe needed no physician to tell him about such phenomena, but the similarity in the physician and the storyteller's use of the language of both medicine and religion to describe the effects of drinking is hardly adventitious within the perspective of Poe's use of medical theory as early as his writing of "Berenice" (1835). Moreover, when Ray himself notes that the phenomena of drunkenness "strongly remind us of some of the manifestations of moral mania" (p. 304), the technical term "moral mania" places the reader in a context that Poe accepts familiarly in the narrator's "unburdening" of his soul.

The narrator, through the remainder of the story, continues to use a similar mixture of language in accounting for what happened. "When reason returned with the morning," the man says, "I experienced a sentiment half of horror, half of remorse, . . . but it was, at best, a feeble and equivocal feeling, and the soul remained untouched." He goes on to tell that the cat slowly recovered, although predictably it fled at the man's approach: "I had so much of my old heart left, as to be at first grieved by this evident dislike on the part of a creature which had once loved me. But this feeling soon gave place to irritation. And then came, as if to my final and irrevocable overthrow, the spirit of PERVERSENESS." Rush, Ray, and other students of mania frequently use the terms "perversity" and "perversion" in discussing the inexplicable actions of patients.[30]

Poe's narrator, however, says equivocally with regard to the "metaphysics" of mania and perverseness: "Of this spirit philosophy takes no account." Poe, nonetheless, develops through the persona the exposition to which so much significance has been ascribed in studies of the man and the work:

> Yet I am not more sure that my soul lives, than I am that perverseness is one of the primitive impulses of the human heart — one of the indivisible primary faculties, or sentiments, which give direction to the character of Man. Who has not, a hundred times, found himself committing a vile or a silly action, for no other reason than because he knows he should *not*? Have we not a perpetual inclination, in the teeth of our best judgment, to violate that which is *Law*, merely because we understand it to be such? This spirit of perverseness, I say, came to my final overthrow. It was this unfathomable longing of the soul *to vex* itself — to offer violence to its own nature — to do wrong for the wrong's sake only — that urged me to continue and finally to consummate the injury I had inflicted upon the unoffending brute.

The exposition prepares for the subsequent behavior: one morning the narrator "in cold blood" slipped a noose about the neck of the cat and hung it to the limb of a tree. In spite of the "cold blood," the narrator says that tears streamed from his eyes and he felt "the bitterest remorse at . . . heart." The pathos — or bathos — is hardly consonant with the taut analysis. It is as if Poe is not quite in control of the imagination that once mastered the most chilling episodes without attributing a mite of sentimentality to the persona. Poe seems to lack psychological distance from the alcoholic subject, even if — or especially if — one reads the cat as symbol of the wife, the witch, the evil woman.

It is not known that Poe ever killed a cat; it is known that he was fond of cats and that one figures poignantly in a description of Poe's poverty in the winter of 1846, not long before his wife's death: Virginia "lay in the straw bed, wrapped in her husband's great coat, with a large tortoise shell cat on her bosom. . . . The coat and the cat were the sufferer's only means of warmth. . . ."[31] It is doubtful that Poe ever could have killed a cat. Yet when the narrator tells of killing one "because I knew that it had loved me, and *because* I felt it had given me no reason of offense . . . *because* I knew that in so doing I was committing a sin," the analysis is Poe's and not without inferences of self-incrimination and helplessness.

The killing of the cat could have been suggested by a case Ray reports in a discussion of "moral mania." Ray describes an impetuous man who was aroused repeatedly to fury by "opposition or resistance": if, for example, "a dog, a horse, or any other animal offended him, he instantly put it to death" (p. 132). Ray introduces consideration of the form of mental disorder by saying that it was little noticed by writers, but, more importantly, in relation to Poe's story, that the disorder tended "to pass into intellectual mania. . . . no less strongly characterized by moral perversities than by hallucinations" (p. 131). Ray also says of moral mania that a very common feature of the disease "is a deep perversion of the social affections, whereby feelings of kindness and attachment that flow from the relations of father, husband, and child are replaced by a perpetual inclination to tease, worry, and embitter the existence of others" (p. 137). Ray further observes that the "ordinary scene of its manifestation is the patient's own domestic circle, the peace and happiness of which are effectually destroyed by the outbreakings of his ungovernable temper and even by acts of brutal ferocity."

Ray's discussion of perversity seems almost casual by comparison with the force and application of the term in Poe's story.[32] Of Poe's statement on perverseness Mme. Bonaparte commented that

> no better description could be given of the counter-compulsions of instinct to the compulsions of morality. . . . Since the instincts and their wild and savage components form the primitive subsoil of the human psyche, Poe was right in asserting "perverseness" — here meant the compulsion to gratify the instincts — to be one of our prime, basic endowments, and to swear it by his similarly endowed soul. [P. 463]

The events described after the killing of the black cat ironically constitute the denouement in Poe's story. The house was destroyed by fire; the narrator was impoverished, resigned himself to despair, habitually frequented the gin houses, and found at one of them another cat closely resembling Pluto. Following the man home, the cat "domesticated itself at once, and became immediately a great favorite" with the narrator's wife. The narrator "soon found a dislike to it arising" within him; "these feelings of disgust and annoyance rose into the bitterness of hatred," and finally "absolute *dread* of the beast."

"This dread was not exactly a dread of physical evil – and yet I should be at a loss how otherwise to define it. I am almost ashamed to own . . . that the terror and horror with which the animal inspired me, had been heightened by one of the merest chimaeras it would be possible to conceive." The chimaera gradually took the image of a gallows the narrator saw marked in white on the breast of the cat. The man was unable to shake off the torments of the hallucination; the moodiness of his usual temper "increased to hatred of all things and of all mankind"; and he blindly abandoned himself to "sudden, frequent and ungovernable outbursts of fury." One day the man's wife accompanied him upon a household errand in the cellar, and the cat followed them down the steep stairs. Nearly throwing the man headlong, the cat exasperated him "to madness." In a surge of wrath he took up an axe, aimed a blow at the animal, but was arrested by his wife. "Goaded, by the interference, into a rage more than demoniacal," he buried the axe in her brain, walled the body up in the cellar, and the guilt of the "dark deed disturbed" him "but little."

Again, ideas for the story are consistent with the account of the consequences of alcoholism by Ray. Describing the disease which often leads to delirium tremens, Ray reports that "under the influence of these terrible apprehensions" the sufferer "sometimes murders his wife . . . whom his disordered imagination identifies with his enemies, though he is generally tractable and not inclined to be mischievous" (p. 302). Ray cites the case of John Birdsell who was tried in 1829 by the supreme court of Ohio on an indictment of murder of his wife. Birdsell had "for several years . . . indulged in fits of intoxication, which, in the later part of the time, had been followed by delirium tremens" (pp. 316-17). Among other details of the case, Birdsell had taken an axe from under the bed and given the fatal blow. Ray also reviews the case of another man who beat out his wife's brains with a stone and "declared he was not sorry for what he had done" (p. 315).

Whatever the personal failures of Poe during the ⌐ ⌐ars of Virginia's illness or the guilt he may have felt, he did not murder his wife, and he testifies that he did not experience delirium tremens until the summer of 1849. The image of the gallows on the cat's breast in "The Black Cat" is a rather contrived, fanciful hallucination and lends credibility to Poe's own record of his *mania à potu*. But Poe's insanity and drinking in the course of his wife's recurring and fatal illness which began in January of 1842, his quitting the job at *Graham's Magazine* in May of 1842 and the subsequent financial difficulties, his tender heart and usually amiable disposition, his self-defeating behavior in spite of his fierce judgment and acumen, his captiousness, the despair he fought against in spite of the fact that he expressed it sometimes analytically and sometimes pathetically — all these tensions must inform "The Black Cat." The painful life in Poe's household and his inordinate failure in coping with it would certainly have been sufficient as a basis for "the most wild, yet most homely narrative" told by a man who says he is "above the weakness of seeking to establish a sequence of cause and effect, between the disaster and the atrocity." The work, however, has its parallels with medical concepts of the period even though Poe no longer had as emphatic need for theoretical sources as he did at the beginning of his career. It should be remembered both that "the instrumentality" for the brutal actions of the persona is "the Fiend Intemperance," and that Poe, in accordance with the medical hypothesis of the period, attributed his own excessive drinking to insanity, the causes of which were undetermined.

I do not think we can conclude that "The Black Cat" is more authoritative in tone than "The Tell-Tale Heart" or "The Man of the Crowd" or "The Fall of the House of Usher." If parts of "The Black Cat" seem less convincing by comparison with the effective and imaginative control of the earlier stories, the development of the concept of perverseness is compelling and radically authentic.

In "The Pit and the Pendulum" (1843, or Christmas, 1842), Poe describes the state of a man condemned to death for offenses that are not articulated: confined to prison at the center of which is a pit "whose horrors had been destined" for the recusant,[33] he fluctuates between "intervals of utter insensibility," "madness," or near annihilation of "his ordinary powers of mind," "the effort to exercise . . . reason," "confusion of mind," "pertinacity of attention," "straining vision," and "shuttering reason" as time and space close in on him. At length "there was no longer an inch of foothold on the firm floor of the prison." Suddenly, as he is on the edge of the pit, a "discordant hum of human voices" signals rescue (H 5:67-85).

There is no confession of crime, nor is there an account of the persona's history, particular temperament, or character. Attention is concentrated on the punishment that the prisoner endures, punishment which is simultaneously real and surreal, physical and psychological. Not the least of the tortures the narrator experiences is "an intolerable thirst." Deriving the decor as well as the images and symbolism from "tales respecting the

[Spanish] Inquisition" and "antique narratives" of dungeons, Poe is the expositor — without a suggestion of medical case or theory — of the agonies of an offending victim. In no other tale does he depict as autonomously and powerfully the conditions or the manifestations of an oppressed consciousness alternating between despair and hope. In no other story does a narrator sacrifice interest in his guilt so that he can focus on his oppression. Poe, the writer, had become his own authority — surely from conscious observation of his own psychological torments.

Yet almost seven years after the publication of "The Pit and the Pendulum," Poe was to write (on July 7, 1849) to Mrs. Clemm that he had been taken to prison "for getting drunk; but *then* I was not. It was about Virginia," and again (on July 19) "I was totally deranged. All was hallucination, arising from an attack which I had never before experienced — an attack of *mania a potu*."

Imagination, Wallace Stevens believed, can help one live one's life, a view close to that of Coleridge who thought that imagination heals. Poe gives no such assurances. The comprehension which he rapidly gained in the depiction of medical concepts and cases provided insight into his own sickness, but neither medicine nor art helped him to endure it very well. And except in "The Imp of the Perverse" (1845), or the satire, he did not turn again for ideas or theories to the metaphysics of mania in the fiction during the years after 1843. If there was ever an enchantment with those subjects or glorification of them in Poe's work, he must have found them wanting in relation to the personal experiences the letters reveal. The evidence suggests, rather, a disenchantment: imagination, Poe might have said to Coleridge or Stevens, can also precipitate one toward one's death. It is hardly beyond the facts of the achievement or the life of Poe to say that as he became increasingly expert in the maniacal subject for which he had such a propensity, and with which he had such a long theoretical, imaginative, and final nullifying acquaintance, he became what he wrote.

If Poe became what he wrote — a case history — in contrast to a customary view that the work was unremittingly autobiographical, the achievement becomes less enigmatic. The failure of readers to make distinctions between biography and art, however, has more than any other oversight complicated the sense of the relationship of Poe's work to his time, his place, and his society.

CONCLUSION

"The pressure of reality," Wallace Stevens has said in *The Necessary Angel* (pp. 22-23), "is . . . the determining factor in the artistic character of an era and, as well, the determining factor of the artistic character of an individual." The nature of that pressure, independent of ideas about it, can never be recovered for an investigation of the determinants of the character of a writer, but the works of the imagination remain intact, and we can at least inquire into the possible sources of their vitality. The inquiries, with the evidence that bolsters them, often enable us to read the works of a writer as an expression which is not entirely or exclusively dependent on the perils of the writer and his personality. Poe's life, which was partially transmuted into poetry and prose, has never been neglected; although it explains much, it has been used to explain too much about the distinctive qualities of his work. An examination of his theory and practice of literature in conjunction with his sense of place and cultural circumstances does not, obversely, account for all the pressures of reality operative in his artistic character. Yet, such an examination contributes, I would hope, to an enlargement of our essential perceptions of that character.

Because it is frequently assumed that the introduction of morbid psychological states into the tales for which Poe is noted depended on personal history or the compulsion for symbolizing an unconscious history, the power of those tales has conditioned many of the ways in which he is read. Evidence of scanty self-awareness in the correspondence with regard to a bout of melancholy or the onset of the secondary alcoholism that troubled him in the period after he discovered the interest in the pathology of mental disease, does not support the view that the psychological tales depended entirely on Poe's observations of himself. His reliance on medical theories to depict mania in the fiction at least raises doubts that the stories are unconsciously autobiographical. In tracing his use of the theories for some of the most authoritative work, one does not explain the causes for his interest in them or the reasons his imagination was emotionally attuned to the subject. I have made no attempt to recapitulate all the arguments of psychoanalytic studies or the disagreements with them; the exponents have had little, if any, knowledge of the history of medical investigation of mania. Moreover, we know less than is believed about the relationships between the mind that imagines and the traumas of the person who chooses from among the primary incidents the materials in which the imagination will invest its energies. Poe himself disclaimed the ability to lay the heart bare.

On the basis of available evidence, as well as the lack of evidence to the contrary, it is possible to say that for the most part the early tales of the grotesque and arabesque were not directly − or consciously − autobiographical. The fact that Poe's first story of mania, "Berenice" (1835), does not have the credibility and coherence of "The Fall of the House of Usher" (1839) shows that the author was groping for mastery of material about which he was initially uncertain and partially informed but imaginative. Moreover, Poe did not begin to go substantively beyond medical theory in the tales of mania until he became attentive to the consequences of the excessive drinking during the middle years of the last decade of his life. If Poe's understanding of perversity, acknowledged as his contribution to the analysis of psychological conflict, is contrasted with an unconvincing image of the alcoholic's hallucination in "The Black Cat" (August 1843), one nevertheless has a measure of the insight of which Poe was capable when he wrote about a subject unquestionably related to his personal history. (He did not, he says in one letter, suffer from hallucinations until the summer of 1849.) On the other hand, the story of a sober young madman in "The Tell-Tale Heart" (January 1843) which seems to have no topical connection with Poe's own disturbances is powerfully realized in terms of both the psychological validity and literary effects. When the primary alcoholism which Poe attributed to insanity developed at an unspecified time, perhaps in 1843, he virtually ceased to write about maniacal states in the language of psychology. A single tale, "The Imp of the Perverse" (1845), completes the group of pieces indebted in large part to Poe's interest in the metaphysics of mania, and it is a variation on the concept of perversity developed in "The Black Cat." Poe was able to write without recourse to medical psychology the surreal images of a tortured victim of the Inquisition in "The Pit and the Pendulum" (1843-44), or the testimonies of hate in "The Cask of Amontillado" (1845) and "Hop-Frog" (1849). He did, however, satirize a current theory of institutional treatment for the mentally ill and refer jokingly to a long acquaintance with the metaphysics of mania in "The System of Dr. Tarr and Prof. Fether" (1845).

The view of Poe as a psychologically alienated, autobiographical writer has repeatedly bound readers to a figure in whose work contradictory evidence has often been overlooked. While other studies have shown Poe's relation to his milieu, none has quite succeeded — nor do I expect to succeed — in breaking the formula which excludes the influence of realities, the natural world, and the democratic society, that shaped the artistic character of his work within the logic of his aesthetic theory. Poe held that the imagination enjoyed a freedom controlled by the text of life — its known qualities — and could not create substantially or at all, but rather combined elements known to the mind. Those collations by comparison with reality were ideal; art *was* the delineation of the ideal; the collations, nevertheless, depended on the elements qua elements perceived, combined, assimilated, and transformed by the intellect in a process analogous to physical chemistry. Such a theory of the imagination could hardly be ascribed to a writer alienated from the world about him.

The reality of the vast, often wild or open, American landscape not only influenced the empty or solitary feeling prevalent in both the poetry and prose, but also provided ambience, images, and metaphors for them. Poe was not a great descriptive poet; writing in a period that preceded the rise of realism, he thought that descriptive poetry was not of the highest order. He was nonetheless sensitive to the expanse of land and sky, to verdant forests and mountains, lone lakes, the flowers, the extremes of light, the magnificence and beauty of the new world. The pleasure he took in natural scenery was consciously sustained and genuinely sustaining in Poe's imagination. Even when he began to tire of its grandeur, he was not necessarily alienated from nature. It is, then, ironic that an experience of a landscape which was important to him and which he repeatedly used — whether he was writing about the paradisal world on a short-lived star or a dream landscape or death's kingdom — has been turned into an evidence for Poe's dissociation from reality. Charles Olson at least saw the experience as a cause for the fact that "Poe dug in," a phrase he would have liked for the predisposition toward psychological phenomena and the study of abnormal states of being. It is likely that radical space, the solitudes, and the restlessness of people born on the American continent encouraged the exploration of the interior world.

The convergence of political and social changes in a new democracy, however, was a more pervasive determinant than the natural landscape for Poe's development as a writer whose subjects were often, but not always, isolated kinds of people and their morbid psychological condition. Even if his most dynamic subject was the solitary self — whether autobiographical or not — there were societal forces that stimulated the interest and the authority Poe brought to bear upon the work he did. A writer whose aesthetic valued the idealization of reality at the same time that the imagination depended on known qualities and elements of reality for substance had to reckon with a society which did not lend itself to idealization as easily as the traditional aristocratic society whose poetry and drama still retain their luminous power. Mutations in content and form were, therefore, inevitable in view of the changing ethos of American culture.

As a native American, Poe, like the foreign observer Tocqueville, was concerned with the consequences of the rise of democracy for literature. The American and the Frenchman held remarkably coincident views to which they seem to have come independently of each other vis-à-vis the historical situation. Evidences in Poe's preference of themes or choices of kinds of work with which to experiment, and in his critical opinions on literature or commentary on related matters, parallel almost point by point Tocqueville's speculative analysis of the sources of literature in the new country. Democracy stimulated the decreation of the imaginative structures of traditional Christianity and ancient cosmologies; democratic peoples, moreover, were not as interested in the past as they were in dreams of the future. In contrast to aristocratic societies whose class system strengthened differences between people, democracy fostered a belief in human equality and similitude that made it difficult to idealize an individual or take any one man in particular as the subject of a literary work. Life itself was apt to be dull, pedestrian, mundane, and circumscribed. The old concepts of tragedy and the tragic hero were gone. Man still survived — man with his dreams, his mystery, his pettiness, and his hidden nerve, his insignificance and anonymity, his passions and terrors, seen for a moment as he wanders on the verge of the abysses of silence. Poe's cultivation of humanity's extreme states of being, as well as his delineation of them in succinct and lucid forms that would catch the imagination of readers who endured prosaic realities, was a replacement for traditional forms of tragedy. His critical theory, the limited range of his work, and particularly "the productions" in which "terror of the soul" is the thesis were not independent of the pressures of cultural change, or inseparable from his awareness of the fact that he was born and lived in a new world. A vast landscape and an ironically restricted free society conspired in the achievements of Edgar Allan Poe, who would be less honored — and less maligned — than he is if he had not explored what he called the caverns of the imagination of man.

NOTES

INTRODUCTION

1. *The Letters of Edgar Allan Poe,* 2 vols., ed. John Ward Ostrom (Gordian Press, 1966), 1: 287.

2. *The Complete Works of Edgar Allan Poe,* 17 vols., ed. James A. Harrison (Thomas Y. Crowell Co., 1902), 8: 276.

3. T. Gilbert Pearson, ed., et al., *Birds of America* (Garden City Publishing Company, Inc., 1936), 2: 53–54, 122–23.

4. Alan Gussow, *A Sense of Place: The Artist and the American Land* (Friends of the Earth and Seabury Press, 1972), pp. 83–84. (Poe's "Silence" was published in 1837; Audubon's *Ornithological Biography,* in 1834.)

5. Horatio Parsons, *The Book of Niagara Falls* (1836), a portion of which is reprinted in John Conron, *The American Landscape* (Oxford University Press, 1973), p. 181. (Poe's story was published in 1841.)

6. Discussion of Poe's concept of the imagination has generally followed Floyd Stovall in "Poe's Debt to Coleridge," *University of Texas Studies in English* 10 (1930): 70–127. Stovall's interest in areas of agreement between Poe and Coleridge is qualified by the view that the American's remarks on the differences between them should be discounted because Poe wanted to make a display of his originality. John Lynen, *The Design of the Present* (Yale University Press, 1969), takes exception: "That the imagination does not create is a significant and inevitable principle within" Poe's system. Lynen is not accurate when he says that the "poet's selecting . . . is no free act of the self," even though he qualifies the point. More important, however, is Lynen's perspective: "To appreciate how radically Poe altered the concept of poetry, one need only survey the consequences of his disagreement with Coleridge. . . . Poe reinterprets the Coleridgean imagination in such a way as to produce most of the changes which separate modern poetry from the Romantic" (pp. 258–59).

7. *The Necessary Angel* (Vintage Books, 1965). See "The Figure of Youth as Virile Poet" (1943), p. 41, and part 1 (originally titled "The Realm of Resemblance") of "Three Academic Pieces" (1947), p. 74. See also *Letters of Wallace Stevens* (Alfred A. Knopf, 1966), ed. Holly Stevens, for Stevens's initial statement that the subject of "realm" was "new and rather quackish," and his later reference to reading Poe's essays, pp. 444, 558. Poe is not mentioned in *The Necessary Angel.*

8. *The Sacred Wood* (Methuen, 1929), pp. 53–54. Eliot is arguing for the "impersonal" theory of composition. Poe is not mentioned.

9. Eliot, in a qualified reassessment of Poe, wrote, "There is little in the work . . . that appears to be based on the landscape and the types of human beings" he knew, but speculates that the "local quality is due simply to the fact that he never had opportunity to travel," and concludes that his "universality comes from writing about what he knew thoroughly." See *To Criticize the Critic* (Farrar, Straus & Giroux, 1965), pp. 54–55. Stephen Spender, commenting on the feeling of primitive horror which rise from the depths of Eliot's poetry, says one is reminded that the southerners Poe and Faulkner were compatriots. See *T. S. Eliot* (Viking Press, 1976), pp. 120–21. Eliot's fragile world is also said to be poised like Poe's "on the brink of dissolution." See Lyndall Gordon, *Eliot's Early Years* (Oxford University Press, 1977), pp. 24, 97.

1: THE AIR OF DEMOCRACY

1. The Henry Reeve text, ed. Phillips Bradley (Alfred A. Knopf, 1945), 2: 78.
2. *The French Face of Edgar Allan Poe* (Southern Illinois University Press, 1957), p. 141.
3. "Editorial Miscellany," *Broadway Journal* (October 4, 1845), in Eric W. Carlson, ed., *Introduction to Poe* (Scott, Foresman and Company, 1967), pp. 517–18.
4. Sidney P. Moss, *Poe's Literary Battles* (Duke University Press, 1969), p. 14.
5. Michael Allen, *Poe and the British Magazine Tradition* (Oxford University Press, 1969), esp. pp. 200–201; and R. D. Jacobs, *Poe: Journalist and Critic* (Louisiana State University Press, 1969).
6. *In the American Grain* (New Directions, 1956), p. 230.
7. Oliver W. Larkin, *Art and Life in America* (Holt, Rinehart, & Winston, 1960), pp. 148–67; John W. McCoubrey, *American Tradition in Painting* (George Braziller, 1963), p. 22; Howard S. Merritt, *Thomas Cole: 1801–1884* (Memorial Art Gallery of the University of Rochester, 1969), p. 16; Robert Spiller et al., *Literary History of the United States* (Macmillan Company, 1955), pp. 210–13; Leo Marx, *The Machine in the Garden* (Oxford University Press, 1967), pp. 142, 192–94; Roy Harvey Pearce, *The Continuity of American Poetry* (Princeton University Press, 1961), pp. 137–40.
8. *Poe: Journalist and Critic*, pp. 154, 138.
9. Floyd Stovall, *Edgar Poe the Poet* (University of Virginia Press, 1969), relates Poe's ideas to transcendentalism, but does not claim they are religiously orthodox. Eric W. Carlson, "Poe's Vision of Man," in *Papers on Poe* (Chantry Music Press, Inc., 1972), ed. Richard P. Veler, concludes that Poe believed " 'each soul is, in part, its own God—its own creator' and thus potentially able to achieve a transcendental 'identity with God' " (pp. 7–20). Patrick Quinn finds Poe devoid of traditional religious convictions.
10. Quotations from poems rely on *Collected Works of Edgar Allan Poe: Poems,* 1 vol., ed. Thomas Ollive Mabbott (Belknap Press of Harvard University, 1969).
11. By contrast, Poe found the scenes of the death of the child Nelly and the uncomprehending despair of the grandfather in Dickens's "Old Curiosity Shop" "so drawn that human language, urged by human thought, could go no farther in the excitement of human feelings. And the pathos is of that best order which is relieved, in great measure, by ideality" (H 10:154–55).
12. "Our Cousin, Mr. Poe," *Partisan Review* 14 (December 1949): 1214–15. See also Daniel Hoffman, *Poe Poe Poe Poe Poe Poe Poe* (Doubleday & Company, 1972), p. 278–99.
13. One minor point is shared by *Eureka* and Tocqueville. Poe comments on a fashion in astronomical treatises: "The force which carries a stellar body around

its primary they assert to have originated in an impulse given immediately by the finger—that is the childish phraseology employed—by the finger of Deity itself" (H 16:253). Tocqueville had said that if poets "strive to connect the great events they commemorate with the general providential designs that govern the universe, and without showing the finger of the Supreme Governor, reveal the thoughts of the Supreme Mind, their works will be admired and understood . . ." (2:80).

14.   W. H. Auden, ed., *Edgar Allan Poe: Selected Prose and Poetry* (Rinehart & Company, 1950), p. ix; and Paul Valéry, *Variety* (Harcourt, Brace and Company, 1927), trans. Malcolm Cowley, p. 130; both reprinted in Eric W. Carlson, ed., *The Recognition of Edgar Allan Poe* (University of Michigan Press, 1966).

15.   Arthur Hobson Quinn and Edward H. O'Neill, eds., *The Complete Stories and Poems of Edgar Allan Poe* (Alfred A. Knopf, 1946) 2: 1083.

16.   *Variety: Second Series* (Harcourt, Brace and Company, 1938), trans. William Aspenwall Bradley, p. 87.

17.   Mary McCarthy, *On the Contrary* (Farrar, Straus and Cudahy, 1961), p. 255.

18.   R. P. Blackmur, ed., *The Fall of the House of Usher and Other Tales* (New American Library, 1960), pp. 382, 379.

19.   Poe once proposed changing the name of the country from "America" to "Appalachia," which would "do honor to the Aborigines, whom, hitherto, we have at all points unmercifully despoiled, assassinated, and dishonored" (H 16:119).

20.   Melville, writing on Hawthorne, may imply a similar point: "'Who in the name of thunder,' would anticipate any marvel in a piece entitled *Young Goodman Brown?*" *The Apple-Tree Table* (Greenwood Press, 1969), p. 81.

21.   Jean Alexander, *Affidavits of Genius* (Kennikat Press, 1971), p. 89; and Arthur Hobson Quinn, *Edgar Allan Poe: A Critical Biography* (Appleton-Century Company, 1941), p. 518. Forgues not only translated but published the first commentary on Poe's stories, and as a result of litigation over one of them stimulated great interest in him in France. See Patrick Quinn, *The French Face of Edgar Allan Poe* (Southern Illinois University Press, 1957), pp. 68–69.

22.   *The Collected Early Poems* (New Directions, 1938), pp. 270–71.

23.   Tamerlane's conflict between love and ambition was probably a typical subject in the period. Emerson, recording topics assigned for the essay meetings of the *Pythologian Society* at Harvard when he was a student, notes for March 26, 1820: "Which is the strongest passion, Love or Ambition?" *Journal*, ed. Edward Waldo Emerson and Waldo Emerson Forbes (Houghton Mifflin and Company, 1909), 1: 40.

24.   Melville's identification of himself as a Virginian may have been his way of paying tribute to Poe, who had just died in October of 1849. Melville started *Moby-Dick* in the summer of 1850; connections with Poe's *Pym* are often pointed out.

25.   See Donald N. Koster, "Poe, Romance and Reality," *American Transcendental Quarterly* 19 (1973): 8–13. Koster, following Roy P. Basler's thesis that the narrator killed Lady Rowena, argues that he also killed Ligeia.

26.   Harold Rosenberg, *The Tradition of the New* (McGraw-Hill Book Company, 1965), pp. 271–72.

27.   In "Fifty Suggestions," Poe writes: "M————, having been 'used up' in the '———— Review,' goes about town lauding his critics—as an epicure lauds the best London mustard—with tears in his eyes" (H 14:174).

28.   John Carl Miller, *Building Poe Biography* (Louisiana State University Press, 1977), p. 208.

2: IMAGINATION OF A GREAT LANDSCAPE

1.   See Roger Forclaz, *Le Monde d'Edgar Poe* (Herbert and Peter Lang, 1974), pp. 121–50; D. E. S. Maxwell, *American Fiction: The Intellectual Background*

(Columbia University Press, 1963), p. 78; and Harry Levin, *The Power of Blackness* (Vintage Books, 1958), p. 104. Arthur Hobson Quinn also gave particular attention to Poe's use of the American scene.

2. Sharon Furrow, "Psyche and Setting: Poe's Picturesque Landscapes," *Criticism* 15 (1972): 16–37; and Darlene Unrue, "Poe and the Subjective Reality," *Ariel* 7 (1976): 66–76.

3. *Collected Poems of Wallace Stevens* (Alfred A. Knopf, 1964), pp. 21–22.

4. I have in mind Jefferson's rotunda at the University of Virginia. A student there, Poe wrote on September 21, 1826, to John Allan: "They have nearly finished the Rotunda–The pillars of the Portico are completed and it greatly improves the appearance of the whole–" (O 1:16).

5. See David Halliburton, *Edgar Allan Poe: A Phenomenological View* (Princeton University Press, 1973), p. 81; and Mabbott 1: 124.

6. *L'Art romantique* (Louis Conrad, Libraire-Editeur, 1925), p. 12.

7. *Poems* (D. Appleton and Company, 1856), 2: 14–15. Other Americans held views similar to those in Bryant's poem. See Leo Marx, chaps. 1–3.

8. *Opus Posthumous* (Alfred A. Knopf, 1957), p. 176.

9. See Robert Morrison, "Poe's 'The Lake,'" *Explicator* 7 (December, 1948): 22; Mabbott 1: 83–84; and *Thomas Moore's Complete Poetical Works* (Thomas Y. Crowell and Company, 1895), p. 129.

10. See James Bruce Eure, *The Swamp Angel* (Exposition Press, 1974), and the photographic essays of Bill Thomas, *The Swamp* (W. W. Norton & Company, 1976), pp. 31–40.

11. Killis Campbell, "Poe's Indebtedness to Byron," *Nation* 87 (March 1909): 248–49; Margaret Alterton and Hardin Craig, *Edgar Allan Poe* (American Book Co., 1935), p. 495; and *The Works of Lord Byron*, ed. Ernest Hartley Coleridge (John Murray, 1905), 4: 131–32, 11–41.

12. Elliot S. Vessell, ed., *The Life and Works of Thomas Cole by Louis Legrand Noble* (Belknap Press of Harvard University, 1964), p. 114. Noble edited Cole's letters and journals, first published in 1853. There was no tradition of American landscape painting before Cole.

13. Oscar W. Larkin, *Art and Life in America* (Holt, Rinehart & Winston, 1960), p. 203, suggests that Cole's allegory "The Voyage of Life" inspired a "golden" landscape passage in Poe's "Domain of Arnheim"; Joy S. Kasson, "'The Voyage of Life': Thomas Cole and Romantic Disillusionment," *American Quarterly* 27 (1975): 42–56, compares Cole's "brooding insight" with that of Hawthorne, Melville, and Poe, the last of whom "was almost exactly Cole's contemporary." Mabbott says the poems "City in the Sea" and "The Valley of Unrest" call "to mind the scenes painted by artists of the Hudson River School, to whom Poe was closely akin in spirit" (p. 346). Richard McLanathan, *The American Tradition in the Arts* (Harcourt, Brace & World, 1968) thinks the fact that Cole was "brought up in the milder more pastoral landscape of England" and came to the United States when he was seventeen may have made him "all the more sensitive to the special qualities of the American scene" (p. 238). Perhaps the five years Poe spent as a child in Britain also made him acutely aware of characteristics of the American terrain.

14. Reproduced in Merritt's *Thomas Cole*, plate 24, p. 75.

15. Lois and Francis E. Hyslop, Jr., trans. and eds., *Baudelaire on Poe* (Bald Eagle Press, 1952), p. 13, from Baudelaire's letter to his mother, 1852, in *Correspondance Générale* (1: 95).

16. Ibid., p. 30, from a letter to Théophile Thoré, art critic, in 1864, *CG* (1: 226).

17. *Les Fleurs du mal: Texte de 1861 avec les variantes de 1857 et des journaux et revues* (Bibliothèque-Charpentier, 1947), p. 310. Theodore de Banville identifies one as a line from "The Haunted Palace" in "L'Héautontimorouménos"; and "Le Flambeau vivant" is Baudelaire's version of themes in Poe's "To Helen." No one, to my knowledge, has noted the connections between "Réve parisien" (pp. 177–79) and Poe's work.

18.   Floyd Stovall says the landscape "has no feature that does not exist in some real landscape" (p. 220); Poe himself contrasts "shallow reverie" and "dreams that have a close semblance of reality" with profound "reverie" (H 14:186–87).

19.   Alvin Rosenfeld, "Description in Poe's 'Landor's Cottage,'" *Short Studies in Fiction* 4 (1967): 264–66.

20.   *Les Rêveries d'un promeneur solitaire,* ed. René-Louis Doyon (René Rasmussen, 1946), pp. 90–101. Eva Rodtwitt and I are the translators.

21.   See F. De Wolfe Miller, "The Basis for 'The Island of the Fay,'" *American Literature* 14 (1942): 135–40; and the disagreement with him by Burton R. Pollin, "Poe's Illustration for 'The Island of the Fay': A Hoax Detected," *The Mystery and Detective Annual* (1972): 22–45, in regard to the engravings adapted to appear with the sketch. See also John Conron's comparison of Poe's "Island" with modes of landscape description in currency during his period (pp. 271–72).

22.   R. D. Jacobs, "Poe's Earthly Paradise," *American Quarterly* 12 (1960): 405–13; Charles Sanford, "Edgar Allan Poe: A Blight upon the Landscape," *American Quarterly* 20 (1968): 54–66; Jeffrey Hess, "Sources and Aesthetics of Poe's Landscape Fiction," *American Quarterly* 22 (1970); 177–89; and David K. Jeffrey, "The Johnsonian Influence: *Rasselas* and Poe's 'The Domain of Arnheim,'" *Poe Newsletter* 3 (1970): 26–29. (The last of Poe's landscape sketches, "Landor's Cottage. A Pendant to 'The Domain of Arnheim,'" was published June 9, 1849; Poe died October 7, 1849.)

23.   Edwin Fussell, *Frontier: American Literature and the American West* (Princeton University Press, 1965), pp. 153, 164; Mabbott 1: 203-4; Christopher Baker, "Spenser and 'The City in the Sea,'" and "Lucretius and 'The City in the Sea,'" *Poe Studies* 5 (1972): 54–55.

24.   Alethea Hayter, in *Opium and the Romantic Imagination* (University of California Press, 1968), observes that the configuration of "strangely lofty and long" halls and chambers that "seem claustrophic" (or "the peculiar horror of limitless yet enclosed space") links Poe's imagery to the effects of opium. She says, however, that some of his "master images, such as a dying girl or a pool of dark water, were based on things he had seen with his own eyes; others, such as a voyage of exploration or a Gothic castle, he derived from books. . . ." Evidence for Poe's addiction "is too uncertain" for one to "tell to which class of images" the characteristic of the opium landscape belongs (pp. 134–40).

3: MERE HOUSEHOLD EVENTS

1.   Joseph Wood Krutch, *Edgar Allan Poe: A Study in Genius* (Alfred A. Knopf, 1926), and Marie Bonaparte, *The Life and Work of Edgar Allan Poe: A Psycho-Analytic Interpretation* (Imago Publishing Company, 1949), trans. John Rodker, examined the relationship between Poe's unconscious drives and literary insight. Napier Wilt, "Poe's Attitude toward His Tales," *Modern Philology* 25 (1927): 105ff., argued against Krutch that Poe "deliberately set out to appeal to the magazine-reading public of his day," a view based on Poe's famous letter stating that "the history of all Magazines shows plainly that those who have attained celebrity were indebted for it to articles *similar in nature* to Berenice," etc. (O 1:57–58). Vladimir Nabokov's *Lolita* (G. P. Putnam's Sons, 1955) parodied Bonaparte's thesis. Daniel Hoffman, in *Poe Poe Poe Poe Poe Poe Poe* (Doubleday & Company, 1972), distinguishes between a story's "technically insane narrator" and Poe's "equally tortured sensibility," but emphasizes his "unflinching honesty" in probing "the recesses of the self" for which the Gothic conventions made available to his imagination those energies "we try to repress" (pp. 258, 298–99, 327). G. R. Thompson, *Poe's Fiction, Romantic Irony in the Gothic Tales* (University of Wisconsin Press, 1973), views Poe as a master of the theories of German "transcendental irony"

rather than the serious Gothic. Preserving some ambiguity as to the real nature of events, Poe's technique "is one of deceptive tripleness: his tales are supernatural on one level, psychological on another, satiric and ironic on another" (p. 77). The vision of the human mind that emerges from the Gothic world "is one of despair over the ability of the mind ever to know anything, either about the ultimate reality of the world or about the mind itself" (pp. 103-4). In *Frontier: American Literature and the American West* (Princeton University Press, 1965), Edwin Fussell conjectures that "so much of [Poe's] terror as was cultural rather than personal–if indeed there exists such a thing as personal trauma unrelated to culture–came from the savage West" (p. 147); the "terror, as well as the poetic sentiment, is identical with the figurative structure of the Western frontier" (pp. 174-75). David Brion Davis, *Homicide in American Fiction* (Cornell University Press, 1957), says that "Poe was not in every way typical of American thought in the 1830s and 40s, but his fascination with villains and murderers, his rejection of rationalism, and his denial of uniformitarianism, all represent the direction in which American thought was moving" (pp. 122-24).

2.   See Edward H. Davidson, *Poe: A Critical Study* (Belknap Press of Harvard University, 1957), esp. pp. 256-57; David Halliburton, *Edgar Allan Poe: A Phenomenological View* (Princeton University Press, 1973), p. 420; and John Lynen, *The Design of the Present* (Yale University Press, 1969), pp. 264, 599.

3.   David K. Jackson, *Poe and the Southern Literary Messenger* (Press of the Deitz Printing Co., 1934), 1: 57-58.

4.   Poe, in an early (1836) review of *Sheppard Lee, Written by Himself* mentions that in the book a mother "becomes melancholy and dies insane," and that the hero, harrassed by pecuniary distress, "falls into a melancholy derangement . . ." (H 9:126-30). The term "melancholy" was commonly used in eighteenth-century medicine. George Cheyne's *The English Malady* (1733) popularized an interest in melancholy, "but his views of mental depression had been largely anticipated" by Nicholas Robinson in *A New System of the Spleen, Vapours, and Hypochondriack Melancholy . . . to which is subjoin'd, A Discourse upon the Nature, Cause, and Cure of Melancholy* (1729), as well as by Sir Richard Blackmore, F. R. C. P., in a *Treatise of the Spleen and Vapours: or Hypochondriacal and Hysterical Affections* (1725). Robinson stressed the unity of mind and body; for him psychological processes were expressions of physical events in nerves. Blackmore was among the first to distinguish severe (or psychotic) depression from mild (or neurotic) ones. See William B. Ober, "Madness and Poetry: A Note on Collins, Cowper, and Smart," *Bulletin of the New York Academy of Medicine* 46 (1970): 229.

5.   Quinn, *Edgar Allan Poe: A Critical Biography* (Appleton-Century Co., 1941), pp. 227-28, and Mabbott, *Complete Works of Edgar Allan Poe: Poems* (Belknap Press of Harvard University, 1969), p. 546.

6.   George E. Woodberry, *The Life of Edgar Allan Poe* (Houghton Mifflin Company, 1909), 1: 154. (Jackson misdates this letter 1837.)

7.   White is writing to Tucker about Poe's review of the novel *Balcombe,* whose author unbeknownst to White was Tucker. The data of the letter is April 26, 1837, after Poe had left the *Messenger;* White felt, he says, "completely gulled" by Poe.

8.   Quinn mistakenly cites this letter as being from White to Minor.

9.   "Madness and Poetry," p. 252.

10.   *Edgar Allan Poe* (Edwin B. Hill, 1933), p. 10.

11.   George Graham wrote of Poe's drinking: "It is true that later in life Poe had much of these morbid feelings which a life of poverty and disappointment is so apt to engender in the heart of man." Graham then discussed the problem of the literary market and said it was small and not profitable for the kind of material Poe wrote. "Hence, when he was fairly at seas, connected with no publication, he suffered all the horrors of prospective destitution; and at such moments, alas! the tempter often

came, and . . . 'one glass' of wine, made him a madman." Graham concluded that "the very organization of such a mind as that of Poe—the very tension and tone of his exquisitely strung nerves . . . utterly unfitted him for the rude jostlings and fierce competition of trade" (Quinn, pp. 663–65).

12. Poe may have considered a similar analysis of the problem as early as July 22, 1845, when he wrote to Dr. Thomas H. Chivers: "There is a topic on which I desire to have a long talk with you. I am done forever with drink—depend upon that—but there is much more to this matter than meets the eye" (O 2:326). Chivers would not have been sympathetic. Of Poe's letter to Eveleth, Chivers wrote:

Suppose a man's wife has ruptured a blood vessel in singing, has that anything to do with insanity? Why, if there is any thing in the world which ought to keep a man in his right sense, it is the consciousness within himself of the duties which he owes his wife in such a case. . . . He drank precisely because he loved liquor—that is all. The latter part of the letter proves what I say *is* so, for he was not cured by his wife's death—nor did it end the oscillation between Hope [sic] and despair or bestow on him so much as the shadow of a new existence—for he died drunk merely three years afterwards! What is anybody to make of all this?

"All this" was from a man who wrote also of Poe's "innocent although unhappy, Bacchanalia." See Richard Beal Davis, *Chivers' Life of Poe* (E. P. Dutton & Company, 1952), pp. 67–68, 2. As a thoughtful contrast to Chivers's view, John Ward Ostrom's lecture on "The Life of Edgar Allan Poe" for *Sound Seminars* (McGraw-Hill Book Co., 1953, reissued by Jeffrey Norton Publishers) traces the alcoholic history in connection with the emotional turmoil, and speculates that the fear and reality of the loss of Virginia is a primary force in the "alcoholic indiscretions." Suffering in the later years from "a form of neuropsychosis" and "cerebral congestion," "intense melancholy, or insanity, as he called it," Poe "approached insanity only when 'his heart was troubled'; when melancholy possessed him, he drank to escape the agonies of it."

13. (Kimber and Richardson, 1812). Rush had earlier included chapters on psychology in *Medical Inquiries and Observations* (J. Conrad and Company, 1805), vol. 1; and had published a discussion of "mental medicine" in *Sixteen Introductory Lectures to Course of Lectures upon the Institutes and Practice of Medicine* (Bradford and Inskeep, 1811). It has been said that Rush coined the term "phrenology" to designate the science of the mind, but this is questionable.

14. Arthur E. Fink, *Causes of Crime: Biological Theories in the United States 1800-1915* (University of Pennsylvania Press, 1938), p. 77.

15. John B. Davies, *Phrenology: Fad and Science* (Yale University Press, 1955), p. ix, cites Alfred Russell Wallace, *The Wonderful Century*. Caldwell's *Elements of Phrenology* (1824) was the "first original publication on phrenology by an American author" [*Phrenological Journal* (1824–25): 113, quoted in Davies, p. 14]. See also Davies, pp. 120–23, and Ernest Hungerford, "Poe and Phrenology," *American Literature* 2 (1930): 209–31, for Poe's interest in the "science." His enthusiasm abated at least near the end of his life, if we judge from the narrator of "The Imp of the Perverse" (1845).

16. *Transylvania Journal of Medicine and Associate Sciences* 5 (1832): 309–50, quoted in Fink, p. 78.

17. (Charles C. Little and James Brown). During his lifetime Ray's book appeared in four subsequent editions; it was last reissued in 1962 (Belknap Press of Harvard University), ed. Winifred Overholser, the text hereafter referred to.

18. *The Life and Work of Edgar Allan Poe: A Psycho-Analytic Interpretation*, p. 213.

19. *Edgar Allan Poe: A Study in Genius*, p. 198.

20. "Monomania" would now read "true paranoia" (Ober, p. 206). The term "mania," in medical as opposed to general usage, is today reserved for symptoms

of the manic phase of a manic-depressive psychosis, characterized by overactivity, pressure of thought, and elevation of emotional tone (A. P. Noyes and L. C. Kolb, *Modern Clinical Psychiatry* [W. B. Saunders, 1958], pp. 161–68, 355–59). In the nineteenth century, however, "mania" was the general term for mental disease; there were, in Ray's system, "Intellectual Mania" and "Moral Mania," either of which might be "general" or "partial" (pp. 104–202).

21. *Medical Inquiries and Observations*, p. 15.

22. David E. E. Sloane, "Gothic Romanticism and Rational Empiricism in Poe's 'Berenice,'" *American Transcendental Quarterly* 19 (1973): 19–26, finds that "the ultimate source" for "the episode of the tooth-pulling" is Rush's "An Account of the Cure of Several Diseases, by the Extraction of Decayed Teeth." Among those cured, Rush cites that of a young man "who had been affected with epilepsy." The "application of a medical cure by Poe's psychologically deranged Romantic hero" becomes, then, "a statement on the dangers of empiricism in an illusory physical world...." Allan Smith, "The Psychological Context of Three Tales by Poe," *Journal of American Studies* 7 (1973): 282–84, notes that "obsession had been described as a principal feature of madness" in Erasmus Darwin's *Zoonomia, or The Laws of Organic Life* (1796), and finds the "defective attention," from which Egaeus suffers, anticipated in a brief general statement from John Abercrombie's notes on insanity in *Inquiry into the Intellectual Powers* (1832).

23. *Sixteen Introductory Lectures*, pp. 386–87.

24. See *Understanding Fiction* (Appleton-Century-Crofts, 1943), pp. 204–5.

25. Leo Spitzer, *Essays on English and American Literature* (Princeton University Press, 1962). Eric W. Carlson, in "Poe's Vision of Man," pp. 17–19, thinks "Usher" is Poe's finest tale, "not merely gratuitous Gothicism." See also David W. Butler, "Usher's Hypochondriasis: Mental Alienation and Romantic Idealism in Poe's Gothic Tales," *American Literature* 48 (March, 1976): 1–12, for significant parallels between the theories of hypochondria (i.e., a melancholic disorder) and romantic qualities of Usher's temperament as well as for Butler's disagreement with I. M. Walker, "The 'Legitimate Sources' in 'The Fall of the House of Usher,'" *Modern Language Review* 61 (October, 1966): 585–92 on Poe's use of medical concepts for atmosphere in relation to the dramatic action of the story. I made the first studies of medical theory as possible sources for a number of Poe's tales; see Edward Wagenknecht, *Edgar Poe: The Man behind the Legend* (Oxford University Press, 1963), p. 60.

26. Arthur Hobson Quinn and Edward H. O'Neill, *The Complete Stories and Poems of Edgar Allan Poe* (Alfred A. Knopf, 1946) 2: 1077.

27. *Sixteen Introductory Lectures*, pp. 280, 386–87.

28. D. E. S. Maxwell, *American Fiction: The Intellectual Background* (Columbia University Press, 1963), p. 81.

29. *The Abnormal Personality through Literature* (Prentice-Hall, 1966), pp. 126–27.

30. Allan Smith, p. 279, points out that "'The Black Cat' is a study of the 'murdering impulse' of the sort noted by Benjamin Rush in his *Sixteen Lectures* (p. 383) by whose account of a famous poisoner of cats it may have been suggested," and that Rush assigns the man to the category of "'perversion of the moral faculty' which seduces a sense to act with it" (p. 440). Ray cites Esquirol's reference to a woman, who after being melancholic for six weeks, was "suddenly seized with the strongest cravings for spirituous drinks, together with . . . agitation, disturbance of mind, and perversions of the affections" (p. 306). Thomas C. Upham, *Outlines of Imperfect and Disordered Mental Action* (Harper and Brothers, 1840), 2: 466, also describes the *"Emergence of suppressed desires in perverted forms:* By a thousand circumstances and in thousands of instances, the feelings are wrenched from their natural position, and shoot forth and show themselves in misplaced and disproportionate forms" etc. (Upham, however, held that moral evil is not the

result of conscious and wilful choice, but has external causes. See David Brion Davis, pp. 21, 294.)

31.   Hervey Allen, *Israfel: The Life and Times of Edgar Allan Poe* (George H. Doran Company, 1927) 2: 722–23. Quoted from reminiscences of Mrs. Gove Nichols in the *Sixpenny Magazine,* February, 1863.

32.   David Brion Davis says Poe "brought a new dimension to the concept of monomania" (p. 108), but "carried romantic philosophy to an extreme" in glorifying "even perverseness and sadism" (pp. 122–23).

33.   The term is Poe's. While it has been observed to be "technically incorrect" within the "historical" frame of the story, Poe's attention is not given to the statutory offenses of the persona but to the tortures he endures.